How to Develop Confident Mathematicians in the Early Years

Showing how everyday experiences can be used to encourage early mathematical thinking, this book will help you to support young children's mathematical development through play.

Developing Confident Mathematicians in the Early Years explains clearly the stages of mathematical development from birth to five years. It considers how practitioners and parents can create a mathematically rich environment and offers a wealth of practical activities and suggestions for adult–child interactions to enhance children's mathematical learning. Features include:

* 60 activities, each covering a core area of mathematical experience – measurement, algebra, data handling, counting and calculation
* clear explanations of the mathematics taking place in each activity and how this forms the foundation for mathematical learning in the future
* practical suggestions for home learning and working in partnership with parents
* links to the EYFS and National Curriculum.

Offering a rich source of ideas using everyday resources, this practical text will inspire practitioners and parents to nurture young children's innate confidence and ability in mathematics.

Tony Cotton taught mathematics in primary and secondary schools for 15 years before moving into teacher education. He became an independent consultant and full-time writer in 2012 but continues to train teachers around the world. He has written many books for teachers and learners of mathematics.

How to Develop Confident Mathematicians in the Early Years

A Guide for Practitioners and Parents

Tony Cotton

Routledge
Taylor & Francis Group

LONDON AND NEW YORK

First published 2019
by Routledge
2 Park Square, Milton Park, Abingdon, Oxon OX14 4RN

and by Routledge
711 Third Avenue, New York, NY 10017

Routledge is an imprint of the Taylor & Francis Group, an informa business

British Library Cataloguing-in-Publication Data
A catalogue record for this book is available from the British Library

Library of Congress Cataloging-in-Publication Data
Names: Cotton, Tony, author.
Title: How to develop confident mathematicians in the early years :
    a guide for practitioners and parents / Tony Cotton.
Description: Abingdon, Oxon ; New York, NY : Routledge, 2019.
Identifiers: LCCN 2018019312 (print) | LCCN 2018029314 (ebook) |
    ISBN 9781315211398 (eb) | ISBN 9780415792790 (hb) | ISBN 9780415792806 (pb) |
    ISBN 9781315211398 (ebk)
Subjects: LCSH: Mathematics—Study and teaching (Preschool) | Mathematics
    teachers—Training of. | Home and school.
Classification: LCC QA135.6 (ebook) | LCC QA135.6 .C6745 2019 (print) |
    DDC 372.7/044—dc23
LC record available at https://lccn.loc.gov/2018019312

ISBN: 978-0-415-79279-0 (hbk)
ISBN: 978-0-415-79280-6 (pbk)
ISBN: 978-1-315-21139-8 (ebk)

Typeset in Optima
by ApexCovantage, LLC

Contents

Contents

Acknowledgements

Five years ago, I became a grandparent. I now have two grandsons and I have learned more about how children learn from having the time and space to observe them than I have from all the conferences I have attended and all the books that I have read. So, this book is for Felix and Tate. The activities that appear in the second half of the book are versions of games that we play and I would invite you to treat them as we do. Not as ways to teach mathematics but as ways to play together and to explore and develop mathematics collaboratively. Listening to each other carefully and revelling in each other's company.

This book started out as a collaboration between Alice Hansen and I. Unfortunately Alice was unable to complete the project but the book is much richer for her input at the early stages.

Thanks also to Helen (or Granny as Felix and Tate call her) who read the early drafts and put them into some sort of order and to Simon Carey for the photography. Simon can be contacted at sdcarey@gmail.com.

Preface

As a parent of three children and more recently as a grandparent, I was fascinated that there was a huge range of books to support parents and carers of young children in developing literacy. In particular these books advise parents and carers how to support young children in developing their skills in reading and becoming lovers of reading. Indeed, the bedtime story is taken as a cultural norm. As a mathematician and a teacher of mathematics, I was equally interested to see very few books exploring early mathematical development in young children. This is despite the fact that all of us who have observed very young children begin to make sense of the world see children using mathematics to come to understand how the world works. This book aims to fill that gap. It is aimed particularly at practitioners working with young children, but I also hope that parents and grandparents will use this book to help them explore mathematics through playful activity with the young children they care for.

When are we engaging with mathematics? The child who sorts out their toy cars into trucks or cars; the child who carefully places their crayons back in their box; the child who fills and empties cups with water; the child who begins to notice numbers on the doors of houses; the child who build towers as tall as they can out of building blocks; all of these children are using mathematics to explore the world. Think about the activity that you engaged in with your own child or grandchild just before bedtime and the bedtime story last night. Or, think about the activity you asked the young learners in your care to finish before you shared a story at 'home-time' yesterday. I can guarantee there was a mathematical element to that activity.

Mathematics involves logic and order. Mathematics involves describing shape and space and creating pattern. Mathematics involves classifying and sorting. You will see in this book how mathematics is embedded in many of our everyday activities and how we can use everyday activities to support young children to become confident mathematicians. Young children, the children you work with or care for, are fantastic at mathematics. They are confident mathematicians. We know that at some stage many young learners lose this confidence. They stop using mathematics to explore unfamiliar situations, stop seeing being mathematical as something everyone can do and something that is as natural as speaking and begin to see it as a challenge, or hard, or even something they are "rubbish" at.

My work in early years settings suggests that some early years practitioners struggle to see the opportunities for mathematical development in activities that they plan. This may be because they, themselves, lack confidence in planning mathematically-rich activities for young learners because they do not see themselves as confident mathematicians. I have yet to hear an early years practitioner tell me that they do not enjoy reading or find writing difficult and boring. Yet, many practitioners will describe their relationship with mathematics in exactly those terms. So, a key aim of this book is to develop early years practitioners' confidence in their own mathematical ability through engaging with young learners in the mathematical activities they will find in these pages. There is no better way to develop our own confidence in a subject, or rediscover our joy in learning, than to engage in playful activity with young children. To see mathematics through the eyes of a four-year-old once again.

We will find it hard to find mathematics in the everyday if we are not used to looking at the world mathematically. One aim of the book is to do just this. The playful activities offered in section 2 of the book make links between day-to-day classroom routines and everyday experiences of young children and use them to develop mathematical thinking.

However, I acknowledge that many are concerned that young children are offered the types of mathematical activities that will prepare them for the next stage of education. Although I hate the term 'pre-school' as it suggests that the purpose of education at this point is simply to prepare children for the next stage of learning rather than being a hugely rich and rewarding educational experience in its own right, I understand the responsibility that practitioners and carers feel to prepare learners for schooling. For this reason, the book also offers suggestions of ways to support children through the transition from their earliest experiences of education into more formal schooling, which is a significant step for many children.

The book is structured around the English National Curriculum and you will find ideas to develop activities drawing on all the mathematics content described in the early years guidance in the book. It is also important to acknowledge the interesting developments in teaching mathematics in the early years globally so you will read about mathematics in Forest Schools in Scandinavia and how mathematical activities are structured thematically in the Primary Years Programme in International schools following the International Baccalaureate programme.

The book is in two sections. The first section explores how we can support young children's mathematical development at a general level. You will come to understand the stages of mathematical development from birth to five-years-old; how to create a mathematically-rich environment in an early years setting or at home; how parent and practitioners can work together to support young children's mathematical development and how we can support young children in successfully negotiating the transition to the next stage of education.

The second section is divided into the core areas of mathematical experience and offers a wide range of activities to support practitioners in planning mathematical activity or carers in extending learning at home through playful activity. There is support for you to understand key mathematical vocabulary in a glossary at the back of the book as well as links to websites, organisations, books and resources which will support you in enhancing young-learners' enjoyment of learning mathematics.

Supporting children's mathematical development

Introduction

This section of the book explains how young children come to develop their mathematical thinking through constructing and building; through negotiating their current understandings with others, through expressing their thoughts and feelings both verbally and symbolically and through actions. I will argue that the adult's role in this is to support children in developing their understanding by providing the possibilities for these activities to take place and through making use of the new skills in the young learner's everyday experiences. The Reggio Emilia approach suggests that a curriculum should be based on the principles of respect, responsibility, and community through exploration and discovery, in a supportive and enriching environment based on the interests of the children through self-guided activities. This section illustrates how these principles and the basic principle of the English Early Years Foundation Stage (EYFS) that every child is a unique learner, can be built on to support young children's development as mathematicians. I will also refer to the New Zealand mathematics framework and the philosophy behind the Forest Schools movement from Scandinavia to set a global context for the discussion.

The Reggio Emilia approach also emphasises that being confused is a major contributor to learning and that young children accept being confused as part of coming to understanding and awareness. I argue that, as early years practitioners, we should expect and allow mistakes to happen and should draw on our learners' interests. Developing and extending those, "Uh?" moments. Our learners with hands upturned, shoulders lifted, eyebrows quizzical, asking, "what's going on here?" This may mean that we begin projects or activities with no clear sense of where they might end, allowing the learners to guide the direction of learning even though that does make planning more complex.

The Reggio Emilia philosophy is based upon children having control over the direction of their learning and learning through experiences of touching, moving, listening and observing. This resonates with one of the guiding principles of the Association of Teachers of Mathematics in the UK, "The power to learn rests with the learner." Reggio Emilia also reminds us that children learn through developing relationships with other children and with material items in the world that they explore together. This would suggest that our role, as practitioners in the early years, is to provide creative starting points and plenty of imaginative materials which encourage our young learners to explore and experiment on their own and with others. For example, a book about a building site might lead to collecting outdoor materials to mix, dilute, build, paint, hammer and sweep.

The EYFS Statutory Framework lays out the requirements for children's learning and development and for keeping them safe in their first stages of education. These requirements cover the seven areas of learning and development which underpin children's activities and experiences for children in early years settings. The framework also contains the Early Learning Goals which summarise the knowledge, skills and understanding that it is hoped children will take with them into primary school. Finally they describe when and how practitioners should assess children's achievements and how they should share these assessments with parents and carers.

Perhaps more importantly the framework describes the four overarching principles that should shape the practice in early years settings. These are that:

1. Every child is a unique child, who is constantly learning and can be resilient, capable, confident and self-assured.
2. Children learn to be strong and independent through positive relationships.
3. Children learn and develop well in enabling environments, in which their experiences respond to their individual needs and there is a strong partnership between practitioners and parents and/or carers.
4. Children develop and learn in different ways and at different rates.

If we are to think about the long-term benefit of implementing these principles in our settings, we can reflect on the fact that the child who is supported to become confident and strong at five will in another five or ten years be more motivated, connected and resilient. These are the creative qualities required by higher education and by employers.

The EYFS also emphasises that all areas of learning and development are important and inter-connected. Young learners do not see the world in terms of discrete subject disciplines and so they should not experience a disconnected curriculum in their early years setting. The EYFS sees the curriculum as containing three prime areas:

*   communication and language
*   physical development
*   personal, social and emotional development

These three areas are crucial for supporting children's curiosity and enthusiasm for learning, as well as for building their capacity to learn. They will do this through having opportunities to experience a language-rich environment which will support them in developing their confidence and skills in expressing themselves; through being active and interacting with others; through physical activity which develops their co-ordination, control and movement, and by developing a positive sense of themselves through forming positive, respectful relationships with others. In addition to this, they will be supported in developing social skills and learning how to manage their feelings. This means they will understand what makes appropriate behaviour when working with others as well as giving them confidence in their own abilities.

As young learners making their way into the world, it is also expected that early years practitioners should support children in the four specific areas of literacy: mathematics; understanding the world; and expressive arts and design.

The EYFS states that literacy development should include encouraging children to link sounds and letters to help them begin to read and write as well as giving them access to a wide range of reading materials such as books, poems, and other written materials to ignite their growing interest in reading and writing. The mathematics they are engaging with should include opportunities to develop and improve their skills in counting, understanding and using numbers as well as calculating simple addition and subtraction problems. They should learn to describe shapes, spaces, and measure. Young children will develop their understanding of the world through being supported in their developing understanding of their physical world and their community through exploration, observation and finding out about people, places, technology and the environment. Finally, expressive arts and design involves enabling children to explore and play with a wide range of media and materials, as well as providing opportunities and encouragement for sharing their thoughts, ideas and feelings through a variety of activities in art, music, movement, dance, role-play, and design and technology.

In planning and guiding children's activities across all areas of learning, it is expected that practitioners should reflect on the different ways that children learn to support them in their planning. The EYFS suggests there are three characteristics of effective teaching and learning and I would argue that these should underpin the mathematical activities we plan for our young learners. Mathematical activities should be designed so that children are:

- **playing and exploring** – whilst engaged in mathematical activity children investigate and experience things. They learn to 'have a go'. This will support them in becoming resilient learners and developing a view of mathematics as something you can explore for yourself rather than be informed about.

- **learning actively**, concentrating and motivated enough to keep on trying if they encounter difficulties. They should also be encouraged to enjoy their achievements and those of their friends.

- **creating and thinking critically**. The mathematics should give children opportunities to develop their own ideas, to make links between ideas and to develop strategies for solving problems.

This approach above is recommended by the government in England. How does this compare with other countries? The curriculum documents from the New Zealand government suggest that mathematics teaching should be seen as a process of inquiry, stating that, "Teaching as inquiry is a useful and integral part of everyday teaching practice" (Education Review Office, 2011). These guidelines remind practitioners that teaching through inquiry is not linear. They also serve as a reminder that we often vastly underestimate young learners' concentration spans. If children are learning through self- and peer-inspired play they can remain focused for long periods of time. This reflects the individual needs of each child as a unique learner. In the New Zealand curriculum this image of each child as a unique learner is highlighted in the document described above which presents the underlying principles of teaching as inquiry. The document opens with these lines:

Ko te Tamaiti te Pūtake o te Kaupapa
The Child – the Heart of the Matter

Moving back to the UK, the Forest School Association in the UK draws inspiration from a movement in Scandinavia which uses the outdoors and the natural environment as inspiration for learning. The Forest School view of learners reflects the overarching principles of the EYFS you were introduced to earlier as well as arguing for all learners' entitlement to a rich learning environment. All learners (and all participants in education are seen as learners) are viewed as:

1. Equal, unique and valuable.
2. Competent to explore & discover.
3. Entitled to experience appropriate risk and challenge.
4. Entitled to choose, and to initiate and drive their own learning and development.
5. Entitled to experience regular success.
6. Entitled to develop positive relationships with themselves and other people.
7. Entitled to develop a strong, positive relationship with their natural world.

(Forest School Association, 2011)

The principles of the Forest School Association also reflect the expectations of the EYFS. They describe the purpose of all learning, including mathematical learning as, "Promoting the holistic development of all those involved, fostering resilient, confident, independent and creative learners" and developing "the physical, social, cognitive, linguistic, emotional, social and spiritual aspects of the learner" (Forest School Association, 2011).

Practitioners can draw on these principles to support planning mathematical activity by using natural resources to support children's developing mathematical understanding and to encourage their natural curiosity. They can link mathematical activities to children's experiences at home in their own play and design activities that build on children's interests. Finally, our planning should build time and space for reflection into all activity so that all learners can understand their achievements and plan for the future.

I hope you can see the close links between the expectations contained in the English Early Years programme and the ideas developed by Reggio Emilia, in New Zealand and in the Forest Schools' movement. These principles inform the book and inform the activities that you will find in section 2. Whilst all three curricula see mathematics as a specific discipline it is also seen as a vehicle through which the areas of communication and language, physical development, and personal, social and emotional development can be strengthened and applied. It should also be seen as closely connected to developing literacy and to supporting the young learners' understanding of the world as well as supporting young children's creativity.

From exploring general principles for learning, let us move on to take a closer look at the current English programme of study for mathematics (DfE, 2017). This states that:

> A high-quality mathematics education . . . provides a foundation for understanding the world, the ability to reason mathematically, an appreciation of the beauty and power of mathematics, and a sense of enjoyment and curiosity about the subject.

This offers us a lens through which to see "high-quality" experiences in our early-years settings or any space in which young children are engaging playfully with mathematics. We will hear our young learners expressing their appreciation of the beauty and power of mathematics. Awe and wonder will be present. We will hear questions being asked and we will see young learners enjoying themselves. John Mason and his colleagues at the Open University (Mason et al., 2005, p. 2) remind us that we should never underestimate the young children that we learn with, saying:

> Expressing generality is entirely natural, pleasurable and part of human sense making. Every learner who starts school has already displayed the power to generalise and abstract from particular cases and this is the root of algebra.

This suggests to me that no-one is more important than the adults young learners spent their time with in their early stages of development. It is these "grown-ups" that support children in becoming confident mathematicians as they move through their educational lives.

There are 4 chapters in this section. Each explores a different aspect to supporting children's mathematical development.

Chapter 1 explains how children develop mathematically from birth to five. The chapter is divided into developmental stages which match the EYFS *Development Matters* stages of development (Early Education, 2012). These are birth–11 months, 8–20 months, 16–26 months, 22–36 months, 30–50 months and 40–60+ months. The overlap between these stages emphasises the difficulty of setting expectations and echoes the principle that children are unique and will develop at different rates.

Chapter 2 gives advice on how practitioners can create a mathematically-rich environment. I hope this will be helpful for early years practitioners creating a learning environment in a setting that is part of a nursery, kindergarten or reception unit in a school and for parents or carers interested in creating mathematically-rich environments at home.

Chapter 3 describes the importance of positive partnerships between early years practitioners and parents or carers in identifying children's learning needs to support their learning and in ensuring a quick response to any specific areas of difficulty. The chapter shows how learning can be extended in the home and how a positive dialogue with parents and carers should be taken into account during any assessment. It also argues that it is vital that all assessments should be shared with parents and carers as they will be able to bring their experience of supporting the child to enhance the results of the assessment. One of the themes in the EYFS is "positive relationships". This emphasises that all key adults a young learner develops caring attachments with have a special role to play in providing an environment in which the children will flourish. These environments are not just classrooms or outdoor spaces rooms at home or recreational spaces children play in but also relate to the positive atmosphere created in warm and caring relationships. Reflecting Reggio Emilia, in these environments, children are respected and valued and their well-being is prioritised. In these environments children feel listened to, which means that they thrive socially and emotionally, as well as developing as mathematicians.

Chapter 4 gives advice to practitioners working with young learners as they prepare for the transition to formal education, including what teachers might normally expect a child beginning primary school in England to be able to do, know and understand. It explains what the Early Learning Goals (ELG) are for mathematics and how reception classes are different to early nursery or kindergarten settings in that they follow the EYFS but also provide a transitional period to the first stages of more formal schooling. It provides advice on helping parents to support their child. A parent or carer might wonder what questions they should ask when they meet their young child's teacher for the first time or what to look for in the new classroom as they visit schools. I hope this chapter might support parents and carers in making informed decisions about the school which might be best for their child. Similarly, it will support practitioners in developing positive relationships with parents and carers from the first time they meet them.

References

Department for Education (DfE) (2017) *Statutory framework for the early years foundation stage: Setting the standards for learning, development and care for children from birth to five.* Available at https://www.foundationyears.org.uk/files/2017/03/EYFS_STATUTORY_FRAMEWORK_2017.pdf (accessed 2 March 2018).

Early Education (2012) *Development matters in the Early Years Foundation Stage (EYFS).* London: The British Association for Early Childhood Education.

Education Review Office (2007) see http://www.ero.govt.nz/publications/directions-for-learning-the-new-zealand-curriculum-principles-and-teaching-as-inquiry (accessed 1 February 2018).

Forest School Association (2011) see http://www.forestschoolassociation.org/full-principles-and-criteria-for-good-practice (accessed 1 February 2018).

Mason, J., Graham, A., Johnson-Wilder, S. (2005) *Developing thinking in algebra.* London: Paul Chapman Publishing.

1 | The developing young mathematician

This chapter describes how young children develop their mathematical understanding, whilst remaining loyal to the principle that every child you will spend time with is a unique individual. They will learn in different ways; be motivated by different activities and contexts for learning. Young children are constantly learning. You know from your experience that they can be resilient, capable, confident and self-assured. The young children we work with do not see the world as compartmentalised into subject disciplines but do understand that mathematics is one of the tools or "languages" with which they can come to understand and act on the world around them.

Before we can unpick how children develop their mathematical understanding we need to come to an agreement about what mathematics is.

What is mathematics?

I want to try and answer this question by analysing and comparing three contrasting curricula and approaches to mathematics in the early years. I will examine the Primary Years Programme (PYP) of the International Baccalaureate programme, the New Zealand approach to mathematics and the English National Curriculum.

Firstly, how does the PYP describe mathematics? The introduction to the scope and sequence for mathematics states:

> The power of mathematics for describing and analysing the world around us is such that it has become a highly effective tool for solving problems. [Learners] . . . can appreciate the intrinsic fascination of mathematics and explore the world through its unique perceptions. . . . [Mathematics] should . . . provide students with the opportunity to see themselves as "mathematicians", where they enjoy and are enthusiastic when exploring and learning about mathematics.

Mathematics is also viewed as a vehicle to support inquiry, providing a global language through which we make sense of the world around us. It is intended that students become competent users of the language of mathematics and can begin to use it as a way of thinking, as opposed to seeing it as a series of facts and equations to be memorised.

(International Baccalaureate Organization, 2009)

This definition of mathematics is set in the context of the aims of the International Baccalaureate (IB) as a whole. Whenever I visit an international school, wherever I am in the world the bullet-pointed list below can be seen displayed in the entrance to the school and on the walls of the classrooms. This includes the kindergarten setting.

The IB programme aims to develop learners who are:

- **Inquirers** through developing their natural curiosity
- **Knowledgeable** through exploring concepts that have local and global significance
- **Thinkers** exercising initiative in thinking critically and creatively
- **Communicators** who understand and express ideas and information confidently
- **Principled** – acting with integrity and honesty
- **Open-minded** – understanding their own cultures and personal histories
- **Caring** – showing empathy, compassion and respect to the needs and feelings of others
- **Risk-takers** approaching unfamiliar situations and uncertainties with courage and forethought
- **Balanced** – understanding the importance of intellectual, physical and emotional balance
- **Reflective** – giving thoughtful consideration to their own learning and experience.

Similarly, the New Zealand curriculum both offers a view of what mathematics is and how this fits into an overall view of the aims of education. The New Zealand Curriculum (Mathematics) offers the following definition:

⬭ Mathematics is the exploration and use of patterns and relationships in quantities, space, and time. Statistics is the exploration and use of patterns and relationships in data. These two disciplines are related but different ways of thinking and of solving problems. Both equip students with effective means for investigating, interpreting, explaining, and making sense of the world in which they live. Mathematicians . . . use symbols, graphs, and diagrams to help them find and communicate patterns and relationships, and they create models to represent both real-life and hypothetical situations.

The curriculum goes on to suggest that mathematics is important as an area of study as it helps learners develop their thinking skills so they can think, "creatively, critically, strategically and logically." They also learn how to interpret and carry out procedures flexibly and accurately and develop communication skills. Particular inquiry skills they can develop through studying mathematics include the ability to create models to fit particular situations and to predict the outcomes of events. They also learn to conjecture and to justify their thinking as well as learning how to estimate and check results for reasonableness.

Finally, all teaching in New Zealand, including the teaching of mathematics should meet the principles of:

- **High expectations:** all learners should be empowered to achieve personal excellence regardless of their individual starting points.
- **Treaty of Waitingi:** all students should understand the inherent connection between and culture and mathematics and the particular culture within which they are growing up.
- **Cultural diversity**: mathematics should reflect cultural diversity and value the histories and culture of all people.
- **Inclusion**: mathematics should be non-discriminatory and inclusive. All learners' identities, languages, abilities and talents should be recognized and affirmed through the curriculum.
- **Learning to learn**: the curriculum should encourage all learners to reflect on their own learning processes and learn how to learn.
- **Community engagement**: the curriculum should connect with learners' wider lives and engage the support of their families and communities.
- **Coherence**: the curriculum should offer learners a broad education that makes links within mathematics itself and between mathematics and other subjects to provide for effective transitions and to open up pathways for further learning.
- **Future focus**: the curriculum should encourage learners to look to the future by exploring issues of sustainability, citizenship, enterprise and globalisation.

You have already met the aims of the English National Curriculum for mathematics in the introduction to this section. Let me remind you of them in more detail. Mathematics is described as:

> ○ . . . a creative and highly interconnected discipline that has been developed over centuries, providing the solution to some of history's most intriguing problems. It is essential to everyday life, critical to science, technology and engineering, and necessary for financial literacy and most forms of employment. A high-quality mathematics education therefore provides a foundation for understanding the world, the ability to reason mathematically, an appreciation of the beauty and power of mathematics, and a sense of enjoyment and curiosity about the subject.
>
> (National Curriculum in England: mathematics programme of study)

Unlike the PYP programme or New Zealand mathematics this is not set within a series of general principles but aims for teachers of mathematics are offered. It is suggested that the teaching of mathematics should ensure that all learners

* **become fluent** in the fundamentals of mathematics, including through varied and frequent practice with increasingly complex problems over time, so that pupils develop conceptual understanding and the ability to recall and apply knowledge rapidly and accurately

* **reason mathematically** by following a line of enquiry, conjecturing relationships and generalisations, and developing an argument, justification or proof using mathematical language

* can **solve problems** by applying their mathematics to a variety of routine and non-routine problems with increasing sophistication, including breaking down problems into a series of simpler steps and persevering in seeking solutions. (My emphasis)

We also have the four overarching principles for early years practitioners. Again, as a reminder, these are:

* every child is a unique child, who is constantly learning and can be resilient, capable, confident and self-assured

* children learn to be strong and independent through positive relationships

* children learn and develop well in enabling environments, in which their experiences respond to their individual needs and there is a strong partnership between practitioners and parents and/or carers

* children develop and learn in different ways and at different rates.

Figure 1.1 Word cloud – what is mathematics?

What can we generalise from these views of mathematics and the aims of teaching mathematics that can help us as early years practitioners? I input the three definitions of mathematics into the application *Wordle* and asked an artist friend to create an image based on this word cloud. (See Figure 1.1)

The image would suggest that mathematics only comes into our presence when we notice it in our worlds. Mathematics comes into existence when we use it and when we use to come to new understandings. This is sense making. There is also a sense of the importance of relationships, both mathematical relationships and relationships between teachers and learners and learners and learners. The phrase "effective problem solving" appears although the disjointedness of the individual words in this phrase suggests to me that this is something which underpins the curriculum rather than forms a discrete part of the curriculum. Figure 1.1 also illustrates that these curriculum documents imply that we learn through exploration of patterns, number and shape and through exploring the mathematics around us.

I repeated the same exercise with the curriculum aims and Figure 1.2 shows the result.

This image has both mathematics and learners at its heart. There seems to be less commonality between the curricula aims. This is unsurprising as both the New Zealand and PYP curriculum aims focus on learner attributes whereas the English curriculum places mathematics at the centre. However, if we had to create a single sentence from the emphases in this image it might be, "Strong children learning and understanding mathematics through exploring problems." We can also pick out the importance of individuals and of encouraging different approaches.

Figure 1.2 Word cloud – aims for teaching mathematics

Where does this leave us? I invite you to create your own definition of mathematics, maybe even work on it with your young learners. Create an image which you can display on the wall in the space in which you work. Make sure you refer to it regularly: relish mathematics, share the enjoyment of coming to understand mathematics with your learners. Most importantly do not become the sort of practitioner who says, "The children loved the session yesterday – they didn't even realise they were doing maths."

Here are my personal definitions of mathematics that I use to make sure I am planning appropriate mathematical activities in my learning spaces which include University lecture theatres, secondary and primary classrooms, early years settings and playgrounds both inside and outside.

We use mathematics to explore and explain the worlds that we live in. These worlds can be social, political or creative. We can apply mathematics to the real world or to our creative and imagined worlds. Mathematics is the exploration of relationships between numbers or shapes; it is classifying and generalizing; it is learning to explore and eventually solve problems – although, sometimes the joy is in the exploration rather than the solution.

Mathematics is learned with and from people who we trust and who we have developed good relationships with. Confidence in mathematics leads to confidence in ourselves and confidence in our judgements. Confidence in mathematics allows us to ask good questions and to become resilient in our approaches to problem solving. We all have individual and creative approaches to learning mathematics. This means we learn most from drawing on peers and teachers who can show us the diverse ways there are to explore mathematics.

Let us move forward, from exploring what mathematics might look like in a general sense to describing and discussing how children come to understand mathematics. In particular, I want to emphasise how children learn through mathematical activity and through solving problems that are of interest to them.

Active learning and mathematics

Think about watching a young child that you know and love exploring the world. You can see them absorbing information, you can see them trying to make sense of things that are happening around them. You will have come to realise that as I write this book I am fascinated by my five-year-old grandson and the way he is learning to become mathematical. As with all very young people he is creating his world and his place in the world and he does this through activity. Let me use a story as an example. Felix has a small elephant watering- can. One of his favourite games is playing with the hosepipe outside, usually to put out imaginary fires and rescue imaginary cats. On this occasion, he put the hosepipe in the 'hole' which is used to fill the watering-can. We waited, he was wondering what might happen, then, suddenly, the water filled the elephant up and spurted out of the trunk. He squealed with delight, "I've made a fountain." He might just as easily have suggested, "I have invented this new thing. I am going to call it a fountain."

Figure 1.3 Elephant fountain

Felix is at his most creative when he is in control of the activity. When he is exploring something that he already has a sense of and pushes it to a new boundary. He bumps up against the limits of his vocabulary and asks for new words to describe the new experience. He uses a story with which he is familiar and sends it off in a new direction. He uses the manipulatives, building blocks, Cuisenaire® rods, magnetic building materials and finds new ways to use them. Or, he uses them in familiar ways to create new activities.

As he becomes more secure in his activity he allows adults into his work, at first just Mum and Dad and Granny and Grandad. He is beginning to allow teachers into this world although they cannot always be trusted. Sometimes they might make suggestions which will bring his narrative to an abrupt end. "No", he will say, "that is not what happened." Felix's creative world and the world he is growing into are indivisible. Action takes place through his creative view of the world. He learns through creativity, through a series of dramatic events. That is not to say that all his learning of mathematics is creative, dramatic or active. Sometimes he just needs something explaining. But all his questions come through his creative interactions with the external world he is experiencing and creating.

Let me use another example. Yesterday we watched a television programme called *Hey Duggee*. 'Duggee' is a scout-master and each episode leads to the 'squirrels' gaining a new badge linked to their experience. This episode was the 'water badge'. It opens with the 'squirrels' trying to explain where water comes from. One suggests that, "Whales make water and spurt it out into the sea." Another says, "The tap makes the water." I asked Felix where he thought water came from. He said, "We make it when have a wee in the toilet and then it goes into the tap." All very imaginative suggestions and all examples of misconceptions. A misconception is a rule or explanation that someone has created to explain something they have noticed. The programme went on to explain the water cycle, in an engaging and accessible way, and after 12 minutes exactly Felix was excitedly explaining how the water-cycle worked to his Granny. Felix had come to a clearer understanding of the world. The important thing in terms of learning is that Felix was in control. He had selected the series he wanted to watch and the episode within this series. It was something that, at this moment, he was interested in.

So, how can we plan for active learning in our early years setting? The first task is to ensure that our learning spaces encourage active learning. The next chapter looks at this issue in depth. For now, use this checklist to help you carry out a quick audit of your setting, or the places in which you play and learn with the children in your care. Are the following available?

Perhaps a more difficult question to answer is, "How can we support child-initiated learning whilst meeting the requirements of the curriculum?" The starting point here, is to remember that active learning does not simply mean that the children are active, it also means that they are in control. This suggests that learners are choosing activities from a range of possibilities. This also allows them to construct and build their learning

---

Auditing my setting

Question	Comment
When planning mathematical activity do I draw on resources which are relevant to the learner's interests and background?	
Are there indoor and outdoor spaces to explore, create and move in and around when engaging in mathematical learning?	
Do I use role-play to support mathematical learning?	
Are there opportunities to learn mathematics in calm and quiet spaces as well as more creative spaces?	

---

on previous experience. Many early years settings use learning stations and ask learners to select an activity. I would suggest that there should not be simply a mathematics station but that mathematics can form a part of the activity at several stations. As you plan these activities, and there are lots of examples in the second part of this book, ask yourself:

- What do I want the students to learn?
- How will the task I have designed help them learn this?
- What prior experience can I expect them to use?
- How does the activity I am planning encourage discussion?
- How does the activity I am planning challenge preconceptions or possible misconceptions?
- What probing questions can I ask to move the students' learning forwards?

If you flick to the second part of the book you will see that this is how I have chosen to present the activities. This is to support you in developing your own subject knowledge. We become confident teachers of mathematics by doing mathematics alongside learners and colleagues.

Problem solving and reasoning in early years mathematics

One of the most influential texts exploring how we come to understand mathematics through problem solving activity is *Thinking Mathematically* by John Mason with Leone Burton and Kaye Stacey, published in 1985 by Pearson Education. They describe the ways that all learners, including the youngest learners search for generality as a way making sense of the world. John Mason and his colleagues have a manifesto. They suggest that:

* Everyone can think mathematically.
* Mathematical thinking can be improved by 'practising reflection'.
* Mathematical thinking is provoked by contradiction, tension and surprise.
* Mathematical thinking is supported by an atmosphere of questioning, challenging and reflecting.
* Mathematical thinking helps in understanding oneself and the world.

I would argue that all these statements can be observed in an early years setting. Young children think mathematically whenever they try to impose order on their world, or whenever they notice a pattern, or compare objects, and all young learners carry out these activities.

Young learners 'practise reflection' through repetition and through the questions they ask. Through this repetition they construct 'schemas', building blocks of knowledge, and use these building blocks to create mental models of the world. You may have noticed a child repeating an action to see if the outcome remains the same. For example, they open a door and notice that the draught from the door means that a balloon blows across the floor. They smile, close the door, move the balloon back to the door and try again. The same thing happens. They repeat again. The next morning, they may try again just to check. They now have a building block, an understanding of a cause and effect.

The third and fourth bullet points give advice as to how we can construct an ethos which will support mathematical thinking and problem solving. We can create a space in which learners come to expect, "contradiction, tension and surprise" and we can support them in developing their mathematical thinking by creating an atmosphere which is questioning and challenging.

Two other ideas which are key to mathematical thinking are *specialising* and *generalising*. At first young learners, in common with many older learners take a 'special' case as true for all cases. For example, if you were to ask your learners to draw you a triangle, I would be almost certain that they would draw an equilateral triangle. We see the special case, a triangle with all sides and angles the same size, rather than the bigger picture. In general, any 3-sided shape is a triangle. Much better to give learners many different types of triangles and ask what is the same about all of these shapes (see Figure 4).

You read earlier in this chapter that one of the aims of the English National Curriculum is to ensure learners will persevere in solving problems This suggests that it is not sufficient to teach children how to solve problems but that we should work with them to develop an aptitude to solve problems and to be resilient when engaged in problem solving activity. Is this how you always feel when you are faced with a mathematical

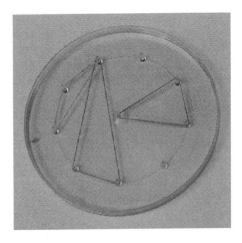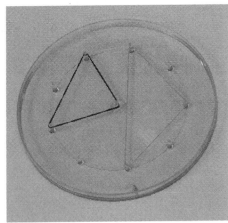

Figure 1.4 Triangles

problem? Do you have the urge to extend problems and find out why certain results are true? Do you persevere if you begin to find things challenging? If not, reflect back on your own learning of mathematics. Did your teachers encourage and support you to develop problem solving skills?

One way that you can develop your own problem solving skills in mathematics, your own mathematical thinking skills, is to explore mathematical problems for yourself alongside the children you teach. In this way you model how problem solving can be open ended. If you show your learners that you enjoy problem solving they will follow your model. Similarly, if you model a systematic and reflective approach to problem solving, articulating your thinking throughout the process, you will offer a great model to your learners. This should include sharing times when you are stuck. Being stuck is an important part of mathematical problem solving.

In an article available on the NRich website based at Cambridge University Sue Gifford describes how early years practitioners can support young learners in becoming confident mathematical problem solvers. She suggests that for the youngest learners the stages of problem solving include finding a way to get started by making sense of the problem for yourself before working on the problem and realising that there is more to the problem than I first thought and exploring further. As we solve the problem we move in cycles before deciding that we have finished, for now, and sharing the solution.

If you reflect on any problem which learners in your care have approached I am sure that you will recognise these stages. Indeed, if you reflect on your own approach to solving a problem you are interested in you will recognise these behaviours in yourself. However, if the problem our learners are presented with is not something they are interested in they will probably simply rush to a solution to get the problem out of the way so they can spend time working at something which does interest them. A huge part of the skill of the early years practitioner is planning activities which will motivate the learners and being flexible enough to know when not to push young children to complete activities if they are not motivated by the problem. This is the difference between encouraging and developing perseverance and trying to force learning to take place. Which it won't.

The same Sue Gifford article alerts us to the increasing sophistication observable in two- and three-year-old children nesting cups and in children aged four- to seven-years-old building a train-track (See Deloache and Brown, 1987). This sense of increasing sophistication in problem solving is described using four stages of development.

1. Brute force: pushing the cups down on each other to try to make them fit or hammering train track pieces together to force them together.

2. Local correction: adjusting one cup or one piece of track which may lead to new problems elsewhere in the stick or in the train-track.

3. Dismantling: realising that the best tactic is to start all over again

4. Holistic review: looking at the problem again and using previous mistakes to take a new approach.

My guess is that you will recognise this list from observing learners you have worked with. I can also think of a few adults who try to apply the "brute force" technique at times! A practitioner's role is to support young learners develop their strategic approach to problem solving. This could include asking appropriate questions such as:

* What are you trying to do? What problem are you trying to solve?
* Have you done anything like this before?
* What do you think you need to solve this problem?
* Why isn't that working?
* What can you try instead?
* Is that better?
* Does it work now? How can we make it even better?
* Can you tell your friends how you succeeded?

Having thought about how mathematical understanding is best developed through activity and through solving problems that are of interest to us we can now move onto exploring the specific skills that will be useful for our learners to develop in order to become effective and confident mathematicians.

What mathematical skills should I be exploring?

My grandson saw a lorry when we went out for a walk yesterday. He could see three wheels on one side of the lorry. He told me, without any prompting, "That lorry has got 6 wheels." He did not expand on this, just stated it as a fact. He did not want to tell me how he knew this and avoided continuing the conversation when we saw a lorry with 4 wheels on one side.

This made me reflect on the notion of 'progression'. I wondered what this experience told me about his 'progress' through the landscape of mathematics. As I have stated earlier, there is a contradiction in the view of progression offered by the English government curriculum guidance. My grandson is currently five, the *Statutory framework for the early years foundation stage* tells those he works with that he should be treated as, "A unique child, who is constantly . . . developing and learning in different ways." When he makes the transition to primary education, next year, his teachers are told by government guidance, that, "The majority of pupils will move through the programmes of study at broadly the same pace." A unique landscape to be explored as an individual has become a journey experienced at the same rate as his peers.

This also begs the question of how should programmes of study be organised and in what order should learners experience mathematical ideas. I recently adapted a series of textbooks from Singapore to follow the Cambridge International curriculum. The two curricula interpret progression differently. In the Cambridge curriculum fractions are introduced gradually, in the Singapore curriculum all unit fractions up to $1/10$ are introduced simultaneously. I wondered why the English curriculum thinks that the notion of $1/2$ is more difficult than that of $1/7$? I also wondered why learners in Singapore do not find it necessary to spend a year learning about $1/2$ and $1/4$ before moving on to divide objects into thirds?

I write this to emphasise that progression in curriculum documents is a sequence which helps us plan, not a sequence that has been specifically designed to support children's learning. Schooling in mathematics expects learning to 'progress at broadly the same pace'. Education in mathematics is when unique individuals develop and learn according to their needs and interests. In the early years we need to try and balance these two approaches. As early years practitioners we should also remember that we should be presenting mathematics in an integrated way. The *Statutory framework for the early years* in England includes the following core experiences for all learners:

> **Communication and language** development involves giving children opportunities to experience a rich language environment; to develop their confidence and skills in expressing themselves; and to speak and listen in a range of situations
>
> **Physical development** involves providing opportunities for young children to be active and interactive; and to develop their co-ordination, control, and movement. Children must also be helped to understand the importance of physical activity and to make healthy choices in relation to food

Personal, social and emotional development involves helping children to develop a positive sense of themselves, and others; to form positive relationships and develop respect for others; to develop social skills and learn how to manage their feelings; to understand appropriate behaviour in groups; and to have confidence in their own abilities

Literacy development involves encouraging children to link sounds and letters and to begin to read and write. Children must be given access to a wide range of reading materials (books, poems, and other written materials) to ignite their interest

Understanding the world involves guiding children to make sense of their physical world and their community through opportunities to explore, observe and find out about people, places, technology and the environment

Expressive arts and design involves enabling children to explore and play with a wide range of media and materials, as well as providing opportunities and encouragement for sharing their thoughts, ideas and feelings through a variety of activities in art, music, movement, dance, role-play, and design and technology.

(Taken from *Statutory framework for the early years foundation stage: setting the standards for learning, development and care for children from birth to five.*)

As we begin to plan mathematical experiences we should ask ourselves how these mathematical activities are contributing to our young learners overall experience of the curriculum.

With thoughts about the contested and complex nature of progression and of mathematics contributing to a cross-curricula experience of learning uppermost, let us look at the expectations in mathematics in the New Zealand curriculum and in the PYP programme.

The sections below are in two parts. Each section of the curriculum is illustrated initially in three tables, one for each of the curricula: the English curriculum, the New Zealand curriculum and the PYP programme. If you teach in England this allows you to compare the expectations in England with other curricula and if you are a carer of a young child in England, you may be interested to see how expectations in England compare with those in other countries. For those of you who teach in a global setting you can decide for yourself what appropriate expectations might be for learners in the early years. You will notice that it is only in England that expectations are related to specific ages.

Children learning number

Last week we were driving up the motorway with our five-year-old grandson in the back of the car. He had got tired of spotting particular types of haulage companies' lorries and looking out for windmills and started counting. Without any prompting (I have realised that Felix has a tendency to become disinterested in an activity if Grandad shows an interest), he announced that he was going to count to 100. Which he proceeded to do. And with impressive accuracy although he skipped the 'eighties'.

Since he has been talking we have named the numbers of all the houses in his street. He lives at number 9 so has heard the pattern 1, 3, 5, 7, 9 many times. Around the corner the pattern becomes 42, 44, 46, 48, 50, 52. He is now recognising these numbers. When he was younger he would point and ask, "what is that one?" This is not to suggest that he has a sense of the 'fiftiness of fifty' but he is recognising patterns and is certainly able to count beyond 20, making his own interpretation of what the pattern of counting numbers might sound like. How does this relate to the expectations in his setting?

The Early Learning Goals for number suggest that by the time he moves into primary school in 6 months' time he should be able to:

○ count reliably with numbers from 1 to 20, place them in order and say which number is one more or one less than a given number. Using quantities and objects, add and subtract two single-digit numbers and count on or back to find the answer. . . . solve problems, including doubling, halving and sharing.

The early mathematical development of young learners is broken down into stages in the document, *Development Matters in the Early Years Foundation Stage* (Early Education, 2012). The document reminds us,

○ Children develop at their own rates, and in their own ways. The development statements and their order should not be taken as necessary steps for individual children. They should not be used as checklists. The age/stage bands overlap because these are not fixed age boundaries but suggest a typical range of development.

The table below (Stages of Development in Understanding Number) shows this breakdown. It includes suggested things that adults can do to support this development. These ideas will be set in the context of wider activities in the second half of this book.

I think it is worth reading through this table and noting which activities you already have planned for as a matter of course, or, if you are a carer for a young person, which activities do you engage in during the day simply regarding them as what you do. Now note which of the suggestions for 'what adults do' you do not do. Why do you think you do not do these things? Is it your own nervousness about mathematics or had you just not thought about the mathematical possibilities for day-to-day activity? I hope you would agree that you can expand your repertoire of everyday mathematical activity to support the developing mathematical understanding of the young learners in your care.

How does this view of mathematics compare to the expectations in young children in New Zealand? The table below shows the suggested progression for children's early understanding of counting.

Stages of development in understanding number.

Age range	What a child is learning	What adults could do
Birth–11 months	Notices changes in number of objects/images or sounds in group of up to 3.	Sing number rhymes as you dress or change babies. Move with babies to the rhythm patterns in familiar songs and rhymes.
8–20 months	Develops an awareness of number names through their enjoyment of action rhymes and songs that relate to their experience of numbers. Has some understanding that things exist, even when out of sight.	Encourage babies to join in tapping and clapping along to simple rhythms.
16–26 months	Knows that things exist, even when out of sight. Beginning to organise and categorise objects, e.g. putting all the teddy bears together or teddies and cars in separate piles. Says some counting words randomly.	Use number words in meaningful contexts, e.g. "Here is your other mitten. Now we have two." Talk to young children about 'lots' and 'few' as they play. Talk about young children's choices and, where appropriate, demonstrate how counting helps us to find out how many. Talk about the maths in everyday situations, e.g. doing up a coat, one hole for each button. Tell parents about all the ways children learn about numbers in your setting. Have interpreter support or translated materials to support children and families learning English as an additional language.
22–36 months	Selects a small number of objects from a group when asked, for example, "please give me one", "please give me two". Recites some number names in sequence. Creates and experiments with symbols and marks representing ideas of number. Begins to make comparisons between quantities. Uses some language of quantities, such as 'more' and 'a lot'. Knows that a group of things changes quantity when something is added or taken away.	Encourage parents of children learning English as an additional language to talk in their home language about quantities and numbers. Sing counting songs and rhymes which help to develop children's understanding of number. Play games which relate to number order, addition and subtraction, such as hopscotch and skittles and target games.

continued

Continued

Age range	What a child is learning	What adults could do
30–50 months	Uses some number names and number language spontaneously. Uses some number names accurately in play. Recites numbers in order to 10. Knows that numbers identify how many objects are in a set. Beginning to represent numbers using fingers, marks on paper or pictures. Sometimes matches numeral and quantity correctly. Shows curiosity about numbers by offering comments or asking questions. Compares two groups of objects, saying when they have the same number. Shows an interest in number problems. Separates a group of three or four objects in different ways, beginning to recognise that the total is still the same. Shows an interest in numerals in the environment. Shows an interest in representing numbers. Realises not only objects, but anything can be counted, including steps, claps or jumps.	Use number language, e.g. 'one', 'two', 'three', 'lots', 'fewer', 'hundreds', 'how many?' and 'count' in a variety of situations. Support children's developing understanding of abstraction by counting things that are not objects, such as hops, jumps, clicks or claps. Model counting of objects in a random layout, showing the result is always the same as long as each object is only counted once. Model and encourage use of mathematical language e.g. asking questions such as "How many saucepans will fit on the shelf?" Help children to understand that one thing can be shared by number of pieces, e.g. a pizza. As you read number stories or rhymes, ask e.g. "When one more frog jumps in, how many will there be in the pool altogether?" Use pictures and objects to illustrate counting songs, rhymes and number stories. Encourage children to use mark-making to support their thinking about numbers and simple problems. Talk with children about the strategies they are using, e.g. to work out a solution to a simple problem by using fingers or counting aloud.
40–60+ months	Recognise some numerals of personal significance. Recognises numerals 1 to 5. Counts up to three or four objects by saying one number name for each item. Counts actions or objects which cannot be moved. Counts objects to 10, and beginning to count beyond 10. Counts out up to six objects from a larger group.	Encourage estimation, e.g. estimate how many sandwiches to make for the picnic. Encourage use of mathematical language, e.g. "Have you got enough to give me three?" Ensure that children are involved in making displays, e.g. making their own pictograms of lunch choices. Develop this as a 3D representation using bricks and discuss the most popular choices.

Age range	What a child is learning	What adults could do
40–60+ months	Selects the correct numeral to represent 1 to 5, then 1 to 10 objects. Counts an irregular arrangement of up to ten objects. Estimates how many objects they can see and checks by counting them. Uses the language of 'more' and 'fewer' to compare two sets of objects. Finds the total number of items in two groups by counting all of them. Says the number that is one more than a given number. Finds one more or one less from a group of up to five objects, then ten objects. In practical activities and discussion, beginning to use the vocabulary involved in adding and subtracting. Records, using marks that they can interpret and explain. Begins to identify own mathematical problems based on own interests and fascinations.	Add numerals to all areas of learning and development, e.g. to a display of a favourite story. Make books about numbers that have meaning for the child such as favourite numbers, birth dates or telephone numbers. Use rhymes, songs and stories involving counting on and counting back in ones, twos, fives and tens. Emphasise the empty set and introduce the concept of nothing or zero. Show interest in how children solve problems and value their different solutions. Make sure children are secure about the order of numbers before asking what comes after or before each number. Discuss with children how problems relate to others they have met, and their different solutions. Talk about the methods children use to answer a problem they have posed, e.g. "Get one more, and then we will both have two." Encourage children to make up their own story problems for other children to solve. Encourage children to extend problems, e.g. "Suppose there were three people to share the bricks between instead of two." Use mathematical vocabulary and demonstrate methods of recording, using standard notation where appropriate. Give children learning English as additional language opportunities to work in their home language to ensure accurate understanding of concepts.

Progression in counting. New Zealand Mathematics Standards.

Key concept	Importance of concept	Teaching and learning points
Pre-counting The key focus in pre-counting is an understanding of the concepts more, less and the same and an appreciation of how these are related. Children at this stage develop these concepts by comparison and no counting is involved.	This is important because these concepts lay the foundation for children to later develop an understanding of the many ways that numbers are related to each other; for example five is two more than three, and one less than six.	Children often have some concept of more; this needs to be extended and refined. Less is a more difficult concept and understanding can be developed by pairing the terms less and more to help develop an understanding of the relationship between the two.
One-to-one counting The key focus of one-to-one counting is developing children's ability to count. Two skills are needed: • ability to say the standard list of counting words in order • ability to match each spoken number with one and only one object	Counting is important because the *meaning* attached to counting is the key conceptual idea on which all other number concepts are based.	Children have often learnt the counting sequence as a rote procedure. They need to learn the meaning of counting by using counting skills in a variety of meaningful situations. Start with counting small numbers, up to five objects. Once children can count reliably their knowledge of the number sequence can be extended to count both **forwards and backwards**, from any given number.
Counting sets The key focus of counting sets is developing children's understanding of cardinality. This means that children understand when you count the items in a set, the last number counted tells the size of that set. They also know that the number in a set will remain constant as long as no items are added to the set, or taken from the set.	Cardinality is important because it allows numbers to be used to describe and compare sets. This allows sets of items to be combined (addition) and separated (subtraction).	Children develop an understanding of cardinality by counting a variety of objects into different sized sets. Counting the same set several times and in a different order develops children's understanding that the number in a set stays the same unless items are added or taken away. The ability to recognise and write numerals are important skills to develop alongside counting.
Counting from one to solve number problems The key focus here is counting objects to solve addition and subtraction problems Children will need to use materials such as buttons, plastic animals, or whatever	Using counting to solve number problems shows children that counting can be used meaningfully in a variety of situations. This helps them understand and	Encourage children to count a wide variety of concrete materials to solve number problems. Start by joining small sets, with a total of five

Key concept	Importance of concept	Teaching and learning points
they may be playing with, to keep track of their counting. For example, children will combine 3 and 2 by first counting out "1, 2, 3" for the first set, then "1, 2" for the second set, then physically join the sets and counting them all "1, 2, 3, 4, 5." **Counting on to solve number problems** Once children understand cardinality and the forward and backward number sequences they can count on or back to solve number problems. For example 5 and 3 can be added by counting on from the largest number: "5. . . .. 6, 7, 8".	appreciate counting as more than a rote procedure. Using counting to combine and separate groups of objects develops children's understanding of the operations of addition and subtraction. Children come to understand that when groups are combined the count gets bigger, and when groups are separated the count gets smaller.	

You will recognise much of the New Zealand curriculum in the Early Learning Goals. There is one big difference. There is no expectation as to how far children will be counting. Rather there is a clear exposition of how children come to learn to count. Indeed the sole expectation for learners understanding of number at the end of Year 1 in school is, "in contexts that require them to solve problems or model situations, students will be able to apply counting-all strategies and continue sequential number patterns based on ones." The story of Felix that opened this section relates much more closely to the New Zealand open view of mathematics than the closed expectations in the English document. Do not forget that the end of Year 1 in New Zealand would be the end of Y1 in England. So, the Early Learning Goals which are aimed at learners who have not yet started primary school have higher expectations than the end of Year 1 in New Zealand. The latest PISA results (2015) for the mathematical understanding of 15-year-olds shows a mean score of 495 for 15-year-olds in New Zealand and a mean score of 492 for their peers in the United Kingdom.

I only raise this point as a way of trying to relieve the pressure on early years practitioners in England or parents and carers who worry that their children, "aren't counting to 20 yet". Don't worry, focus on developing the counting strategies outlined in the New Zealand curriculum and described in more detail below.

Before we move on I want to explore the expectations within the Primary Years Programme used in many international schools. As in both the English and New Zealand curriculum the "scope and sequence", as it is called, is accompanied by a disclaimer.

Whilst the mathematical skills are presented as a continuum and suggest a form of progression, practitioners are reminded that:

- There are stages of learning that precede those in the scope and sequence.
- No two learners will follow the same pathway through any continuum.
- Learners of the same age will have a wide range of understanding of the same mathematical idea.
- Learners will display understandings from across several phases of learning at once. This is not unusual.
- The continuum should not be seen as a fixed progression. Practitioners should not expect learners to completely understand ideas in one phase before they explore ideas in another phase.

The first phase of learning for PYP programmes has the overall expectation for number that:

> Learners will understand that numbers are used for many different purposes in the real world. They will develop an understanding of one-to-one correspondence and conservation of number, and be able to count and use number words and numerals to represent quantities.
>
> (International Baccalaureate Organization, 2009)

Again, this expectation does not bring with it an upper or lower limit for counting and using number words. Of course, many children enter the early years of education able to count, or at least they can recite numbers names in order. They will also be aware of numbers. They will have been introduced to numbers as a way of describing how many things there are in a set. They may not understand the concept of cardinal numbers yet, that is when we use a number to label a set. They will have seen numbers which act as a way of describing position, the number on a house for example, the order of pages in a book. This way if using numbers is called ordinal numbers. We do not use these numbers to count. Finally, they will have come across numbers which simply act as labels, the numbers on a bus for example. This does not mean the bus is the thirteenth to leave the garage that morning or it was the thirteenth bus to be given a route; it is simply a way of knowing whether or not you should get on the bus. So, knowing that numbers can be used different ways let us focus on counting.

Rochel Gelman and Randy Gellistel published a book entitled *The Child's Understanding of Number* in 1986. This has been used by many practitioners to understand how we learn to count. Gelman and Gellistel suggested there are five principles which underpin counting. These are:

1. **The one-to-one principle:** When a child first begins to count they will often say number names, not necessarily all the names and not always in the same order. A

child who understands the one-to-one principle realizes that we only count each item once. We can model this by touching items as we count them. This is directly linked to:

2. **The stable order principle**: There are not many series of words that we always report in the same order. A child who understands the stable order principle understands that to count we always say 'One, two, three, four . . .' and so on. This is a series of words whose order remains the same if we want to count.

3. **The cardinal principle:** This means that we understand the last number we say when we are counting a set if objects tells us how many objects there are in that set. That is why we tend to emphasise the last number we say when we are counting objects with a young learner.

4. The **abstraction principle**: I can count five cars. Then I can count four lorries. If I count them all together I can count nine vehicles. So, a child that understands the abstraction principle knows that we can count anything – they do not all have to be the same type of object.

5. **The order irrelevance principle**: You will have experienced a child counting a set of objects, arranged in a line, and carefully and accurately telling you confidently that there are five. You then move the objects, so they are not in a line and ask how many there are. The child looks confused and them counts them again, showing surprise when there are, again, five objects. When we understand the order irrelevance principle we understand that we can count a set of objects starting with any object in the set and we will always get the same answer.

We can use these principles to build on the experiences that young learners bring with them and use the ideas in the table, 'Stages of Development in Understanding Number' to ensure all learners engage with numbers in a wide-ranging and motivating way to both describe situations and to solve problems.

Children learning measures

Felix and I used to spend a lot of time building towers when he was about three years old. To be honest we still enjoy building towers, now pretending it is to entertain his younger brother. He used to get a small stool and my task was to hand him the large connecting blocks so that he could build one that was taller than he was. I would ask, "Can you reach?". He would smile and nod, reaching ever higher. Then he would say, "You have to do it Grandad – it's too reachy." Young children develop a sense of measurement as comparison well before we see them in our early years setting. They understand which object might appear longer, although they do not always match up the ends. They know that they can lift some things and other things are too heavy. They understand when one object will fit inside another. And they will have learned all this through exploration and activity. The Early Learning Goals suggest that:

> ⭕ Children (should) use everyday language to talk about size, weight, capacity, position, distance, time and money to compare quantities and objects and to solve problems.

Our job as practitioners is to continue to plan activities that will allow our young learners to explore measures. There will, of course, be children who are not fortunate enough to have had these experiences at home; our task here is too ensure all learners experience activities involving measurement in the same spirit of activity and discovery. The table below offers more specific ideas. I have adapted the table from the Early Learning Goals because 'shape, space and measures' is subsumed into one area in the document. We will discuss 'shape and space' in the next section.

I think the most important thing to remember is that people learn how to measure by measuring. Sometimes we learn this by observing. We learn to bake and cook by watching someone we love and respect baking and cooking and by working alongside them. We learn to put up shelves or carry out more complex constructing work by working alongside someone and gradually taking on more responsibility. Activities in school can mirror this. Build, measure, compare and explore using measures alongside the learners. Introduce them to the language of measure by using appropriate terms consistently,

Stages of development in measures.

Age range	What a child is learning	What adults could do
Birth–11 months	Babies' early awareness of measure grows rom their sensory awareness and opportunities to play and explore.	Provide a range of objects of various textures and weights in treasure baskets to excite and encourage babies' interests.
8–20 months	Recognises big things and small things in meaningful contexts. Gets to know and enjoy daily routines, such as getting-up time, mealtimes, nappy time, and bedtime.	Play games that involve curling and stretching, popping up and bobbing down. Encourage babies' explorations of the characteristics of objects, e.g. by rolling a ball to them.
16–26 months	Enjoys filling and emptying containers. Associates a sequence of actions with daily routines. Beginning to understand that things might happen 'now'.	Talk to children, as they play with water or sand, to encourage them to think about when something is full, empty or holds more. Help young children to create different arrangements in the layout of road and rail tracks. Highlight patterns in daily activities and routines.

continued

Age range	What a child is learning	What adults could do
22–36 months	Beginning to categorise objects according to properties such as shape or size. Begins to use the language of size. Understands some talk about immediate past and future, e.g. 'before', 'later' or 'soon'. Anticipates specific time-based events such as mealtimes or home time.	Use descriptive words like 'big' and 'little' in everyday play situations and through books and stories.
30–50 months	Uses positional language.	Demonstrate the language for measures in discussions, eg. long, longer', 'longest', 'short', 'shorter', 'shortest', 'heavy', 'light', 'full' and 'empty'. Find out and use equivalent terms for these in home languages. Encourage children to talk about the shapes
40–60+ months	Can describe their relative position such as 'behind' or 'next to'. Orders two or three items by length or height. Orders two items by weight or capacity. Uses everyday language related to time. Beginning to use everyday language related to money. Orders and sequences familiar events. Measures short periods of time in simple ways.	Ask 'silly' questions, e.g. show a tiny box and ask if there is a bicycle in it. Be a robot and ask children to give you instructions to get to somewhere. Let them have a turn at being the robot for you to instruct. Encourage children to use everyday words to describe position, e.g. when following pathways or playing with outdoor apparatus.

show your multilingual learners that you respect their family's background be learning key vocabulary in their home language. Learn alongside the children. Develop displays both as posters and as collections and label these. Use the mathematical vocabulary to develop reading and writing skills. Let us look again to New Zealand. How is progression in understanding measures described for young children there?

Here you can see more clearly the movement from describing attributes, "That is a tall tower"; to making direct comparisons, "That tower is taller than me". Then on to making indirect comparisons, "That tower is bigger than mummy." (Even though mummy is not in the room) and finally measuring using units. At first, "That tower is 15 bricks high" and then later measuring in centimetres using a ruler. You can imagine a similar progression for all the different facets of measuring: length, weight, capacity, money and time.

Measurement: early learning progression in New Zealand.

Key concept	Importance	Teaching and learning points
Identifying the attribute: The key focus of this step is helping children to become aware of the physical attributes of objects in order to clearly identify what is to be measured.	This is important because children need to have an understanding of length, volume and weight as attributes of objects before they can meaningfully compare and measure these attributes.	To develop these understandings, children need opportunities to explore objects and their attributes and to discuss these experiences with others. They also need to be introduced to appropriate descriptive language such as big, heavy, tall and empty.
Direct comparison: The key focus of this step is to directly compare the attributes of two or more objects to establish, for example, which is longer, heavier or holds more. When comparing three or more objects they can be ordered.	This is important because comparison is needed to meaningfully describe length, weight and volume. For example, to say "my pencil is long" does not have a lot of meaning, but to say "my pencil is longer than yours" is meaningful.	Considerable time may have to be spent on these experiences for children to become aware of what can be done to an object without changing the quantity of the attribute that is being investigated.
Indirect comparison: The key focus of this step is to indirectly compare objects when it is not possible to place them together directly. For example, children can measure around the bottom of a sand volcano using string and then compare the length of the string with the distance around the base of another volcano to find out which is longer.	This is important because indirect comparison provides a useful way to measure. For example, we can use a piece of string to measure the width of the door and then hold the piece of string against a table to see if it will fit through the door.	This method of measuring is useful only when the objects that need to be measured cannot be compared directly. Look for situations like this in children's play and use these to introduce and explore indirect comparison.
Using something to measure: The key focus of this step is to use ordinary objects to measure. Suitable objects are usually known to children and readily available. For example steps or hands can be used to measure length, and cups measure volume. Anything used to measure in this way can be described as a unit.	Units of measure are important because without them questions such as "How much more does this jug hold?" cannot be answered. Using an object to measure also introduces many of the principles associated with successful measurement. These include: Measures are expressed by counting the total number of units used.	Encourage children to place units end to end as gaps or overlaps between the units will result in inaccurate measurements. Estimation is a useful skill to introduce alongside measuring with objects. This can be developed by asking children to guess how many cups of water will fit into the jug before they carry out their measurement.

continued

Key concept	Importance	Teaching and learning points
	Units of measure need to be chosen appropriately. For example, the length of the room could be measured by hand spans but a pace is more appropriate.	Using a unit requires that children are able to count and understand that the last unit counted gives the measure of the object.
	During a measurement activity the unit must not change.	It is useful to measure the same object with different units to help children understand you need a smaller quantity of larger units to measure an object or vice versa.
	Measurement provides opportunities to strengthen both children's number and measurement understandings at the same time.	

Something you will notice is that not all children will match the ends of two objects they are comparing. This is easy enough to model: Take a very short piece of ribbon, giving a child a much longer piece and say, "My ribbon is longer than yours." They will protest and then 'prove' your assertion by placing the ribbons next to each other as shown in Figure 1.5.

They will protest and explain to you that you have to line the ends of the ribbons up to be fair. Similarly, you can struggle to lift up an empty cardboard box, with great dramatic effect you can pretend it holds a huge weight. Then ask the child to lift it. "But it's really light" they will exclaim. They have learned that you can't judge the mass of an object by its size. These are two examples of misconceptions around conservation of measures. This means that the length of a pencil doesn't change when you move it and that the volume of water in a glass remains the same even when you pour it into another container.

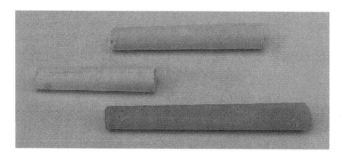

Figure 1.5 Comparing lengths inaccurately

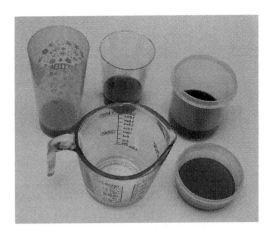

Figure 1.6 Conservation of volume

The first phase of learning about measuring in the PYP scope and sequence document suggests that:

> ◯ Learners will develop an understanding of how measurement involves the comparison of objects and the ordering and sequencing of events. They will be able to identify, compare and describe attributes of real objects as well as describe and sequence familiar events in their daily routine.

This expectation is exemplified through two learning outcomes.

> When constructing meaning, learners:
>
> 1. understand that attributes of real objects can be compared and described, for example, longer, shorter, heavier, empty, full, hotter, colder
> 2. understand that events in daily routines can be described and sequenced, for example, before, after bedtime, story-time, today, tomorrow.

Again, in the PYP scope and sequence we can see children coming to an understanding of measurement through measuring things and talking about what they are discovering.

▨ Children learning shape and space

I have been a member of the Association of Teachers of Mathematics (ATM), in the UK since I first started teaching in 1981. One of the guiding principles of the ATM says:

> ◯ The ability to operate mathematically is an aspect of human functioning that is as universal as language itself. Attention needs to be drawn to this fact constantly. Any possibility of intimidating with mathematical expertise is to be avoided.

I have already described how Maria Montessori describes young learners as having 100 languages and how I see one of these languages as the language of mathematics. I hope I have been drawing your attention to this throughout the book. I also hope that you have not felt intimidated by the mathematics that is contained in the book. That final sentence is what particularly drew me to the guiding principle above more than anything else.

The learners in the large secondary school in the North of England where I started my career had spent a large part of their time being intimidated by mathematics to the extent that they decided they were not capable of thinking mathematically. Indeed, if they were successful in any of my lessons, which they were, they would decide that what I was introducing them to could not be mathematics. Mathematics, for them, was defined as that stuff they couldn't do.

I recently commissioned a very successful sculptor and graphic artist to create a graphic for a mathematics journal I edit. I asked him to read through the articles and create an image which summarised his response to the articles. When we met he said he felt unable to this as he could not understand all the articles. He said, "I loved the articles about geometry and using pattern but I couldn't understand the one about prime numbers, so I stopped thinking." For him, it seemed, the articles exploring shape and space were not "proper" mathematics in the way that prime numbers are. He was intimidated by mathematics, or by what he perceived as "real" mathematics.

I tell these stories to try to adjust your metaphor for the world of mathematics. If you currently see mathematics as a staircase or a ladder and the aim in learning mathematics is to ascend this ladder as it disappears into the clouds, erase this image. Instead, imagine a map of a large country. This country contains many different areas to explore and you can discover many routes around the country. One of the main counties in this country is called 'shape and space' and this is just as important a part of the country as the county called 'number'. People who live here and who spend time here are just as much members of the mathematical community as people who spend all their time in 'number'.

What might you find in your exploration of this fascinating place? The table below will start to fill in the map.

These activities lead us to the Early Learning Goal, "[Children] recognize and describe patterns. They explore characteristics of everyday objects and shapes and use mathematical language to describe them." This appears to make an early years practitioner's job very straightforward: provide children with the opportunity to observe and create patterns and to describe the world they observe using the language of shape and space. Does the New Zealand curriculum give us more clues as to how we might do this?

The centre of the experience here is noticing what is the same and what is different about objects. As we describe shapes and objects that we see, holding and moving them we begin to use mathematical vocabulary. As we classify shapes and objects we use this

Progression in learning shape and space.

Age range	What a child is learning	What adults could do
Birth–11 months	Babies' early awareness of shape and space grows from their sensory awareness and opportunities to observe objects and their movements, and to play and explore.	Provide a range of objects of various textures and shapes in treasure baskets to excite and encourage babies' interests.
8–20 months	Recognises shapes in meaningful contexts.	Encourage babies' explorations of the characteristics of objects. Talk about what objects are like and how objects, such as a sponge, can change their shape by being squeezed or stretched.
16–26 months	Attempts, sometimes successfully, to fit shapes into spaces on inset boards or jigsaw puzzles. Uses blocks to create their own simple structures and arrangements.	Use 'tidy up time' to promote logic and reasoning about where things fit in or are kept. Help children use their bodies to explore shape, through touching, seeing and feeling shape in art, music and dance.
22–36 months	Notices simple shapes and patterns in pictures. Beginning to categorise objects according to properties such as shape. Begins to use the language of shape.	Talk about and help children to recognise patterns. Draw children's attention to the patterns e.g. square/oblong/square which emerges as you fold or unfold a tablecloth or napkin.
30–50 months	Shows an interest in shape and space by playing with shapes or making arrangements with objects. Shows awareness of similarities of shapes in the environment. Shows interest in shape by sustained construction activity or by talking about shapes or arrangements. Shows interest in shapes in the environment. Uses shapes appropriately for tasks. Beginning to talk about the shapes of everyday objects, e.g. 'round' and 'tall'.	Demonstrate the language for shape, position and measures in discussions. Find out and use equivalent terms for these in home languages. Encourage children to talk about the shapes they see and use and how they are arranged and used in constructions. Value children's shape patterns, e.g. helping to display them or taking photographs of them.
40–60+ months	Beginning to use mathematical names for 'solid' 3D shapes and 'flat' 2D shapes, and mathematical terms to describe shapes. Selects a particular named shape. Uses familiar objects and common shapes to create and recreate patterns and build models.	Play peek-a-boo, revealing shapes a little at a time and at different angles, asking children to say what they think the shape is, what else it could be or what it could not be. Introduce children to the use of mathematical names for 'solid' 3D shapes and 'flat' 2D shapes, and the mathematical terms to describe shapes.

Learning progression in understanding shape and space. New Zealand curriculum.

Key concept	Importance	Teaching and learning points
Objects the same The key focus of this step is to help children become aware of the features or attributes of objects by finding objects that are alike.	This is important because looking for objects that are alike helps children become aware of their features, for example size or number of sides. Once children can recognise these features they can then use these to describe and sort objects.	Children begin by using their own vocabulary to describe objects. For example they may find two objects that are "pointy", "big" or "like a house". Informally introduce names for 2- dimensional shapes and 3- dimensional objects as opportunities present themselves.
Objects the same and different The key focus of this step is to encourage children to sort objects into groups that are alike and different. As they do this they are encouraged to think about the features of 2-dimensional shapes and 3- dimensional objects.	Sorting is important because it helps children to understand that objects can be grouped on the basis of their similarities. These understandings will later develop into knowledge of the different classes of 2-dimensional shapes and 3-dimensional objects and their properties.	It is important that children have experience with a rich variety of 2- and 3- dimensional shapes. Provide children with a variety of objects to sort; use both shape blocks and more informal materials such as buttons, bottle tops, boxes and containers. Asking children to re-sort a collection will encourage them to attend to a variety of features. For example, "I love the way you've sorted these into colours. Now let's sort these red ones."
Classifying objects The focus of this step is developing the understanding that groups of objects share features. For example, objects can be grouped by the number of sides or faces that they have.	This is important because 2 and 3 dimensional shapes are classified on the basis of their features. For example, all cubes have 6 faces and 8 corners (vertices). Classifying shapes into groups and describing these helps children develop these understandings.	In any sorting activity the children, not the educator, should decide how to sort. This ensures children use attributes they understand for sorting and provides the educator with an opportunity to observe known attributes. Children can then be encouraged to focus on unknown attributes to extend their knowledge. As children develop their understanding of classes of shape they will benefit by representing these through drawings, words, constructions and dramatisations.

mathematical vocabulary to justify our different classifications. It is important that early years practitioners become confident in using mathematical vocabulary about shapes themselves. Introduce the mathematical names for shapes as soon as children start to notice and describe them. If you do not know the name of a shape don't worry, look it up and be as excited as your young learner when you discover what it is called. This focus on noticing and describing properties of shapes as we classify them is mirrored in the PYP scope and sequence document (International Baccalaureate Organization, 2009). The expectation for phase 1 is:

> Learners will understand that shapes have characteristics that can be described and compared. They will understand and use common language to describe paths, regions and boundaries of their immediate environment.

The accompanying learning objective is:

> When constructing meaning learners: understand that 2D and 3D shapes have characteristics that can be described and compared . . . [using a common language].

I hope that this section gives you the confidence to plan activities involving noticing, sorting, classifying and describing shapes and that you are beginning to see mathematics as much more than simply counting.

Children learning algebra

Overt discussion of the exploration of algebra, both in terms of numbers and shapes, does not appear in the Early Learning Goals or the New Zealand curriculum apart from general statements about exploring and noticing number patterns. However, I think algebra is worth separating from the areas above so that we can focus on the specific algebraic skills that children are developing as young learners. You will notice that I have deliberately not used the phrase 'pre-algebra'. My view is that if young learners are coming to understand ideas which can be described as algebra then they are doing algebra.

In the article, 'Algebra in the Early Years? Yes', Jennifer Taylor-Cox argues for the inclusion of algebra in the early years curriculum. She describes how, in the United States, algebra acts as a gate-keeper for access to universities and higher education. In the UK I think many learners see algebra as symbolising all that is challenging about mathematics. If you understand algebra you belong to that special group of people who are 'good at mathematics'. So, what does algebra in the early years look like?

The moment we start to notice patterns and either describe them or continue them we are thinking algebraically. This might be patterns of shapes or staircases built using

Cuisenaire® rods (see Figure 1.7). If we notice a general rule that we can use to describe a pattern we are using algebra to describe the world.

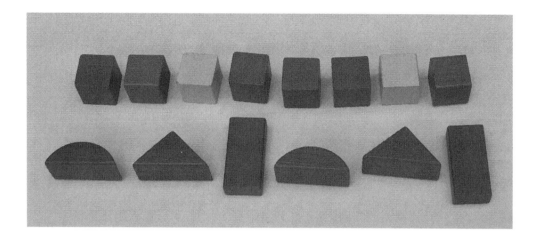

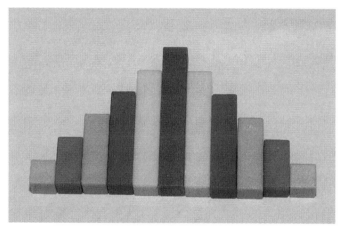

Figure 1.7 A repeating shape pattern and Cuisenaire® staircases

When you use balance scales (see Figure 1.8) to compare masses of objects you are exploring algebra. A young learner may discover that three rolls of tape balances two lemons or that four toy cars balance two lorries.

Encourage your young learners to record these relationships in any way they wish. As they do this they are writing equations. The only one of the three curricula we have been exploring which describes algebra separately is the PYP scope and sequence document. They have a section titled, 'Pattern and Function' (International Baccalaureate Organization, 2009). The expectation for Phase 1 is that,

Learners will understand that patterns and sequences occur in everyday situations. They will be able to identify, describe, extend and create patterns in various ways.

This is exemplified through this learning objective:

When constructing meaning learners: understand that patterns can be found in everyday situations, for example, sounds, actions, objects.

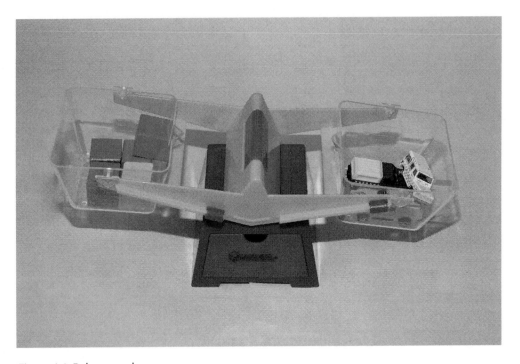

Figure 1.8 Balance scales

Again, we see, that mathematics in general, and in this case, algebra in particular is something that happens all the time, all around us. Our main task is to notice and share the mathematics that is all around us.

In a nutshell

1. Young children use mathematics to describe the world and to explore their worlds.

2. Mathematics is best learned through activity and through solving problems we are interested in. Mathematics should be planned across the curriculum and can be used to develop understanding in other curriculum areas.

3. Do not focus on a linear view of progression. See mathematics as a landscape to be explored with learners at different points in this landscape.

4. Comparing expectations across international curricula suggests that we should focus on the process of developing mathematical understandings rather than measuring fixed outcomes.

5. Young children are able to develop algebraic understandings.

References

Deloache, J. S. & A. L. Brown (1987) The early emergence of planning skills in children, in J. Bruner and H. Haste, *The child's construction of the world*. London: Methuen, 108–30.

DfE (2017) *Statutory framework for the early years foundation stage: Setting the standards for learning, development and care for children from birth to five.* Available at https://www.gov.uk/government/uploads/system/uploads/attachment_data/file/596629/EYFS_STATUTORY_FRAME-WORK_2017.pdf (accessed 2 March 2018).

Early Education (2012) *Development matters in the Early Years Foundation Stage (EYFS)*. London: The British Association for Early Childhood Education.

Gelman, R. and Gallistel, R. (1986) *The child's understanding of number.* Cambridge, MA: Harvard University Press.

Gifford, S. Mathematical problem solving in the early years: Developing opportunities, strategies and confidence. Available at https://nrich.maths.org/12166 (accessed 2 March 2018).

International Baccalaureate Organization (2009) Primary Years Programme. *Mathematics scope and sequence.* https://www.ic.edu.lb/uploaded/programs/IB_PYP_Program/PYP_math_scope_and_sequence.pdf (accessed 7 February 2018).

New Zealand Mathematics http://nzcurriculum.tki.org.nz/The-New-Zealand-Curriculum/Mathematics-and-statistics (accessed 7 February 2018).

Taylor-Cox, J. (2003) Algebra in the early years? Yes. *Young Children*, January, 14–21.

2 Creating a mathematically-rich environment

Think, for a moment, about a time when you really felt you were learning. When you were exhilarated by the progress you were making, when you discovered something new and exciting, when something you thought you were certain about was challenged and you had to adjust the way you thought about the room. Put yourself back in that place, with those people and try to bring that sense of inspiration to the front of your mind.

* Where were you?
* Were you inside or outside?
* What was the weather like – what about the decoration in the room?
* What equipment were you using?
* What resources were available?
* What 'things' could you see around you?
* Who were you with?
* Who was inspiring you? Supporting you? Challenging you? Questioning you?

These are all questions about the learning environment and you have just re-imagined what makes a rich learning environment for you. This chapter explores what it is that makes not just a rich learning environment but a mathematically-rich learning environment. There is much in common with the learning environment you have just imagined but there are also things which are specific to create the conditions for learning mathematics.

A mathematically-rich environment consists of three inseparable parts: people, spaces and objects. We will explore each of these areas in this chapter and discuss the particular role they play in creating a mathematically-rich environment. I will return to the Early Learning Goals in England to develop the ideas contained there about developing a mathematically-rich environment linked to the specific areas of mathematics. But first we need to agree that the environment matters.

Why does the environment matter?

A philosopher called John Rawls offers us a way to explore why we might want to create a rich learning environment and the changes we might make to the current environment to enhance it. He described a thought experiment called "the veil of ignorance". I would like to invite you to take part in this experiment. Sit somewhere where you are alone, close the door and the curtains or shutters. The experiment goes like this:

The outside world has now completely changed. Society has been reinvented and new rules apply. When you leave the room, you could have taken the place of any person in society. In my case, I could now be one of the two homeless men camping up on the old railway line in the town in which I live; I could be the owner of the coffee-shop next door or one of the waiters; I could be the town mayor; I could be the old lady who was knocked down crossing the road yesterday; I could be the new-born baby I saw on her mother's front on my morning run.

If this new society is socially just I would have no concerns about the role I would take in the new society. I could be confident that my needs would be taken care of and that I would be able to lead a good and fulfilled life.

How can this thought experiment help us think about our early years setting or the spaces we share with young learners we care for? I invite you to think about the children in the current setting you work in. Would you be perfectly happy for a child that you love to exchange places with any of the children in your setting? If not, what would you change about the environment, about the people, the spaces and the objects to create an environment that would be better suited for the children that you feel are currently disadvantaged? The power of this thought experiment is that it gives us the power to act. The learning environment is something that we have some control over. Did you think about the changes you might want to make in terms of the people? That is the starting point for our discussion of creating a mathematically-rich environment.

People in a mathematically-rich environment

The definition of an enabling environment in *Development Matters* (Early Education, 2012) states:

> Children learn and develop well in enabling environments, in which their experiences respond to their individual needs and there is a strong partnership between practitioners and parents and carers.

It goes on to say that enabling environments value all people and value all learning. So, a first step towards developing a mathematically-rich environment is that positive relationships between adults are clear to the children and to all who visit the setting. Ideally children will experience a diversity in the adult population, there will be female and male role models. There will be a range of practitioners from the same diverse backgrounds as the population of the country in which you work and learn. If your setting struggles to recruit practitioners who reflect diversity it is important that you draw on the local community resources to broaden the diversity within the setting.

What skills and understandings might we expect adults in the setting to display if they are to add to the richness of the environment? *Children Thinking Mathematically: Essential Knowledge for Early YearsPractitioners* (DCSF, 2009) lists four important characteristics. The document suggests that mathematically-rich environments are supported by practitioners that:

- share positive beliefs about young children learning mathematics.
- are aware of the mathematics that arises through children's self-initiated play.
- have high expectations of young children's mathematical understanding.
- understand babies' and young children's mathematical development, learning from reflecting on observations and through discussions with their team, and use this knowledge to 'tune into' the mathematics that children explore within their play.

I often use this list as an aide-memoire for colleagues working in the early years asking them to reflect honestly. If we take the time to observe young children engaged in mathematical activity we cannot fail to become aware of the mathematics that naturally arises through self-initiated play. It really is only a matter of looking for it. My aim is that through using the activities in the second half of the book you will become adept at noticing the mathematics and that once you have started noticing mathematics in self-initiated play you will not be able to un-see it. It is also though noticing the mathematics within children's play that you will be able to share your positive beliefs with the children. You will have to ration yourself to the number of times you say, "What an amazing piece of mathematical thinking."

The final two bullet points do demand a bit of work on our behalf, and summarise why I wanted to write this book. I think all early years practitioners are brilliant at planning and supporting activities across most of the curriculum. I am not convinced that all practitioners are confident enough in their own mathematical understanding to challenge young learners thinking and or to understand mathematical development. Hopefully, if you have already read Chapter 1 in this section, you are feeling more confident. I am sure that by the time you have engaged in the type of mathematical activity described in section 2 of this book you will have high expectations of all the young children you work with and be able to see the mathematical learning that is taking place. This type of adult is described in *Children Thinking Mathematically* as someone who:

> ⬭ Value[s] children's ideas and support[s] children's play and mathematical explorations through collaborative dialogue help to 'scaffold' children's thinking. Practitioners can help children go beyond what they already understand and can do. Thinking, making meanings and understanding are significant aspects of mathematics.

The people in a mathematically-rich environment also see children's learning as a partnership between the setting and the home environment. Chapter 3 explores this partnership in much more detail but for now we should note that any mathematically-rich environment would include practitioners talking with parents about their children's developing understanding of mathematics. My ideal environment would also include practitioners, parents and children all actively exploring mathematics together.

Before we move on to think about creating mathematically-rich spaces in which to learn together let me revisit the grids in *Development Matters* (Early Education, 2012) which chart mathematical development from birth to the start of primary school. These grids include a column outlining what a rich environment for learning mathematics might look like. As in the previous chapter I have divided the curriculum into number, shape and space, and measure.

Mathematically-rich environments for learning number

Age	What a child is learning	What a rich environment could provide
Birth–11 months	Notices changes in number of objects/images or sounds in group of up to 3.	Display favourite things so that a young baby can see them.
8–20 months	Develops an awareness of number names through their enjoyment of action rhymes and songs that relate to their experience of numbers. Has some understanding that things exist, even when out of sight.	Provide a small group of the same objects in treasure baskets, as well as single items. Create a mobile, occasionally changing the number of items you hang on it. Collect number rhymes which are repetitive and are related to children's actions and experiences. Use song and rhymes during personal routines. Collect number and counting rhymes from a range of cultures and languages.

continued

Continued

Age	What a child is learning	What a rich environment could provide
16–26 months	Knows that things exist, even when out of sight. Beginning to organise and categorise objects Says some counting words randomly.	Provide varied opportunities to explore 'lots' and 'few' in play. Equip the role-play area with things that can be sorted in different ways. Provide collections of objects that can be sorted and matched in various ways. Provide resources that support children in making one-to-one correspondences, e.g. giving each dolly a cup.
22–26 months	Selects a small number of objects from a group when asked, for example, "please give me one", "please give me two". Recites some number names in sequence. Creates and experiments with symbols and marks representing ideas of number. Begins to make comparisons between quantities. Uses some language of quantities, such as 'more' and 'a lot'. Knows that a group of things changes in quantity when something is added or taken away.	Make a display with the children about their favourite things. Provide props for children to act out counting songs and rhymes. Provide games and equipment that offer opportunities for counting, such as skittles.
30–50 months	Uses some number names and number language spontaneously. Uses some number names accurately in play. Recites numbers in order to 10. Knows that numbers identify how many objects are in a set. Beginning to represent numbers using fingers, marks on paper or pictures. Sometimes matches numeral and quantity correctly. Shows curiosity about numbers by offering comments or asking questions. Compares two groups of objects, saying when they have the same number. Separates a group of three or four objects in different ways, beginning to recognise that the total is still the same.	Give children a reason to count, e.g. by asking them to select enough wrist bands for three friends to play with the puppets. Enable children to note the 'missing set', e.g. "There are none left" when sharing things out. Provide number labels for children to use, e.g. by putting a number label on each bike and a corresponding number on each parking space. Include counting money and change in role-play games. Create opportunities for children to separate objects into unequal groups as well as equal groups. Provide story props that children can use in their play,

Age	What a child is learning	What a rich environment could provide
	Shows an interest in numerals in the environment. Shows an interest in representing numbers. Realises not only objects, but anything can be counted, including steps, claps or jumps.	
40–60+ months	Recognise some numerals of personal significance. Recognises numerals 1 to 5. Counts up to three or four objects by saying one number name for each item. Counts actions or objects which cannot be moved. Counts objects to 10, beginning to count beyond 10. Counts out up to six objects from a larger group.	Provide collections of interesting things for children to sort, order, count and label in their play. Display numerals in purposeful contexts, e.g. a sign showing how many children can play on a number track. Use tactile numeral cards made from sandpaper, velvet or string. Create opportunities for children to experiment with a number of objects, the written numeral and the written number word. Develop this through matching activities with a range of numbers, numerals and a selection of objects.

Reading this table carefully we begin to form a picture of the environments in which a learner will be able to explore their developing mathematical understandings. There will be objects in baskets and boxes which learners can use to sort and to build whilst an adult notices what is the same and different and counts alongside the young learner. The space will be filled with the sounds of counting rhymes and stories in a range of languages.

There will be numbers used as labels around the setting. There will also be number lines which include zero both on the wall and on the floor. Children will hop on the number line on the floor counting as they do.

There will also be a range of games using dice and spinners which encourage young-learners to explore number as they play these games. There will be mathematics-specific resources for young learners to explore such as *Numicon*® and *Cuisenaire*® *rods*. Young learners will also be choosing to use tablets to explore number using apps such as *Touchcounts*. (See Appendix 3 for fuller descriptions of resources available.)

Many of these same resources can be used to ensure the environment is rich for developing an understanding of measuring. As we have already discussed developing an understanding of measurement relies on a developing understanding of number. An example might be the development of the role play area into a shop with money and calculators.

Mathematically-rich environments for learning measures

Let us begin with an adapted version of the table from *Development Matters* (Early Education, 2012).

Age	What a child is learning	What a rich environment could provide
Birth–11 months	Babies' early awareness of shape and space grows from their sensory awareness and opportunities to observe objects and their movements, and to play and explore.	Provide a range of objects of various sizes in treasure baskets to excite and encourage babies' interests. Look at books showing objects such as a big truck and a little truck; or a big cat and a small kitten. Use story props to support all children and particularly those learning English as an additional language.
8–20 months	Recognises big things and small things in meaningful contexts. Gets to know and enjoy daily routines, such as getting-up-time, mealtimes, nappy time, and bedtime.	
16–26 months	Enjoys filling and emptying containers. Associates a sequence of actions with daily routines. Beginning to understand that things might happen 'now'.	Provide different sizes and shapes of containers in water play, so that children can experiment with quantities and measures.
22–26 months	Beginning to categorise objects according to properties such as size. Begins to use the language of size. Understands some talk about immediate past and future, e.g. 'before', 'later' or 'soon'. Anticipates specific time-based events such as mealtimes or home time.	Provide opportunities for children to measure time (sand timer), weight (balances) and length (standard and non-standard units). Vary the volume and capacity equipment in the sand, water and other play areas. Use coins for sorting in role play areas. Measure for a purpose, such as finding out whether a teddy will fit in a bed.
30–50 months	Shows interest in shape by sustained construction activity or by talking about relative size.. Shows interest in measures in the environment.	Play games involving children positioning themselves inside, behind, on top and so on. Provide rich and varied opportunities for comparing length, weight, capacity and time. Use stories such as *Rosie's Walk* by Pat Hutchins to talk about distance and stimulate discussion about non-standard units and the need for standard units.

Age	What a child is learning	What a rich environment could provide
40–60+ months	Can describe their relative position such as 'behind' or 'next to'. Orders two or three items by length or height. Orders two items by weight or capacity. Uses everyday language related to time. Beginning to use everyday language related to money. Orders and sequences familiar events. Measures short periods of time in simple ways.	Make books about measures: long and short things; things of a specific length or comparing things that are heavier or lighter. Have areas where children can explore the properties of objects and where they can weigh and measure, such as a cookery station or a building area. Plan opportunities for children to describe and compare measures and distance. Provide a range of natural materials for children to arrange, compare and order.

How has our environment developed so we can resource a rich-environment in which young-learners develop their understanding of measures? There are still boxes and baskets of objects to sort and count but we also begin to notice and to support learners as they describe them using the language of measure. They sort using criteria such as big, middle-sized and small; light and heavy; tall and short.

There are clocks in the setting, so we can refer to the time of day and there are displays which refer to the times of the day or ordering events and books which tell the story of the passing of time. There is a cooking station and a construction area, both everyday activities which demand measurement. As in the previous chapter I have chosen to split the early years curriculum outlined in *Development Matters* (Early Education, 2012) into 'measures' and 'shape and space' whereas the document puts the two areas together. Of course, all the areas of mathematics overlap and it is important that practitioners make the connections between the different areas.

Mathematically-rich environments for learning shape and space

Here the treasure baskets and boxes have been expanded to include shapes the young learners can use creatively whilst adults play with them naming the shapes and noticing their properties. Young learners come to an understanding of the properties of shapes by describing them to their peers or to adults. They learn the language of shape by hearing adults naming the shapes. It is important that you are not embarrassed about using the correct mathematical names for shapes as soon as children begin to play with them.

Age	What a child is learning	What a rich environment could provide
Birth–11 months **8–20 months**	Babies' early awareness of shape and space grows from their sensory awareness and opportunities to observe objects and their movements, and to play and explore.	Provide a range of objects of various textures and shapes in treasure baskets to excite and encourage babies' interests. Look at books showing shapes and patterns. Use story props to support all children and particularly those learning English as an additional language.
16–26 months	Attempts, sometimes successfully, to fit shapes into spaces on inset boards or jigsaw puzzles. Uses blocks to create their own simple structures and arrangements.	Use pictures or shapes of objects to indicate where things are kept and encourage children to work out where things belong. Provide different sizes and shapes of containers in water play, so that children can experiment with quantities and measures. Offer a range of puzzles with large pieces and knobs or handles to support success in fitting shapes into spaces.
22–26 months	Notices simple shapes and patterns in pictures. Beginning to categorise objects according to properties of shape. Begins to use the language of shape.	Display patterns from a variety of cultures.
30–50 months	Shows an interest in shape and space by playing with shapes or making arrangements with objects. Shows awareness of similarities of shapes in the environment. Shows interest in shape by sustained construction activity or by talking about shapes or arrangements. Shows interest in shapes in the environment. Uses shapes appropriately for tasks. Beginning to talk about the shapes of everyday objects, e.g. 'round' and 'straight'.	Organise the environment to foster shape matching, e.g. pictures of different bricks on containers to show where they are kept. Show pictures that have symmetry or pattern and talk to children about them.

Age	What a child is learning	What a rich environment could provide
40–60+ months	Beginning to use mathematical names for 'solid' 3D shapes and 'flat' 2D shapes, and mathematical terms to describe shapes. Selects a particular named shape. Uses familiar objects and common shapes to create and recreate patterns and build models.	Make books about shape in the environment. Plan opportunities for children to describe and compare shapes. Provide materials and resources for children to observe and describe patterns in the indoor and outdoor environment and in daily routines. Provide a range of natural materials for children to arrange and compare.

Mathematically-rich spaces

Have a look round your setting or the rooms at home where you interact and play with the young learners in your care. To what extent do they reflect the kind of spaces described above. Are there different spaces, or stations, to support young learners developing mathematical understandings? Spaces for baking? Spaces for making and construction? Is there easy access to scrap materials which can be used to create new objects for the creative and fantasy worlds that young children operate in?

Elisabeth Carruthers and Maulfry Worthington (2003) describe the importance of mark-making in supporting learners' mathematical understandings. This will also be evident in a mathematically-rich environment. This means there should be resources which allow children to make marks. Easily accessible whiteboards or flip-charts which only the children write on. This means they own these recording spaces and do not have to use teacher-owned resources such as the white-board or flip-chart on the carpet area. There will be examples in the setting of children's records of mathematical activity. This should be their own choice of marks and their own choice of layouts which represent their mathematical thinking.

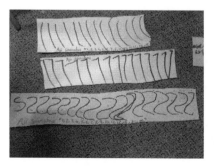 

Figure 1.9 Children's mathematical mark-making

You have perhaps noticed that I have chosen not to separate 'inside' and 'outside' spaces. This is because I think that all activities that are available inside should be available outside and that children should be moving between the indoor and outdoor environment freely. Of course, the outdoor environment gives lots of opportunities for extending mathematical thinking. There is space for much bigger number-lines to be painted on the ground and on the walls. We can build very tall towers out of large construction materials. We can use water and sand to explore volume without worrying about making a mess indoors. Perhaps most importantly we can go for walks and notice shapes, sizes and numbers in the environment. If we model the outdoor environment of the setting we work in as mathematically rich then the whole world becomes mathematically rich for our young learners.

In a nutshell

1. Mathematically-rich environments are formed by spaces, people and objects.

2. People in mathematically-rich environments share positive beliefs about children learning mathematics and have high-expectations of children's mathematical understanding

3. Mathematically-rich environments draw on everyday resources to support children's mathematical development.

4. Mathematically-rich environments should be developed inside and outside the spaces in an early years setting.

References

Carruthers, E. and Worthington, M. (2003) Research uncovers children's creative mathematical thinking, *Primary Mathematics*, Vol. 7/3 (Autumn).

DCSF (2009) *Children thinking mathematically: PSRN essential knowledge for early years practitioners*. Nottingham: DCSF.

Early Education (2012) *Development matters in the Early Years Foundation Stage (EYFS)*. London: The British Association for Early Education.

3 Parents as partners

I used to collect my two sons from their primary school every Friday. They lived with their mum during the week and used to stay with me at weekends. The first primary school they attended had a strict policy about parents. They had to stay outside the school grounds and wait for the children to come through the gate. One day, there had been an after-school event and the children were collected from the classroom. On our way out of the school we crossed a line painted on the floor. My sons pointed this out as the line that parents were not allowed to cross. We spent several mischievous moments jumping over the line before my sons lost their nerve and we ran out of the playground.

The next primary school they attended was a small village school. The first time that I collected them myself, their step-mum and step-sister were all invited into the classroom so that their classmates could be introduced to their "Leicester family". We genuinely felt that home and school came together at that moment, and that alternative homes were acknowledged and seen as important.

This chapter considers why close working between early years practitioners and the parents and carers of young learners is vital for the identification of children's learning needs and to ensure a quick response to any area of particular difficulty. We will explore how learning can be extended in the home, as well as how the dialogue between practitioners and parents and carers should be taken into account during assessment and how all assessments should be shared with home. This chapter draws on both the "Positive relationships" themes of the Early Years Foundation Stage and the document *Building Partnerships between Parents and Practitioners* published by *Aistear* in the Republic of Ireland. This document forms a part of the curriculum framework from birth to six in the Republic of Ireland.

The discussions will take particular note of the place of mathematics learning and teaching in these partnerships. I wonder if sometimes we do not explore the way that such partnerships can develop to support the learning of mathematics as we all feel nervous about our own abilities and understand the importance of the subject in making judgements about our children's futures.

Firstly, we should consider why such partnerships might be important.

Why are partnerships between home and early years settings important?

In 1975 the English government at the time set up an independent committee to explore the teaching of language in an increasingly multicultural and multilingual educational environment. A sentence which appeared on page 294 of the report became a mantra across the schools in Leicester where I was working ten years after the report was published.

> No child should be expected to cast off the language and culture of the home as he (sic) crosses the school threshold (and).... the school should adopt a positive attitude to its pupils' bilingualism and whenever possible should help maintain and deepen their knowledge of their mother-tongues.
>
> (DES, 1975, p. 294)

If we replace the words "language", "bilingualism" and "mother-tongues" with "mathematics" we have the perfect rationale for partnerships between parents and carers and practitioners in early years settings. The children we work with come to school full of mathematical experiences and practitioners can draw on these experiences to enrich the mathematics on offer in the setting. As practitioners we learn about these experiences through discussions with the young learners and their parents and carers. It is sometimes easy to forget that the children we learn alongside in an early years setting spend the large proportion of their time outside this setting.

Through working with parents and carers in partnership we increase the number of teachers available to our young-learners. We know that not all young-learners have the same support from home. The careful developments of partnerships with all parents and carers can begin to reduce this inequality. All those involved in raising young children have a right to be as involved as possible in every aspect of their child's life, even if an adult's own experience in education was negative. This may be particularly relevant for mathematics. A practitioner in an early years setting may be able to offer support to parents and carers in developing their own understandings of mathematics, and this positive experience may have a long-lasting effect on the adult's new relationship with formal education.

A partnership only exists where there is genuine two-way communication with both partners listening carefully and valuing what the other partner has to say. Many schools have drawn on the idea of "unconditional positive regard" developed by the psychologist Carl Rogers. This does not mean that we have to like every adult that we come across in our day-to-day interactions but does mean that we have to listen very carefully to what they say and to try and understand their point of view, particularly in regard to a child that we are teaching (in partnership).

The document from *Aistear* that I introduced you to earlier contains a useful table (p. 8) which summarises the benefits of such positive partnerships. I have slightly adapted the table and reproduce it below.

I imagine most people reading this book are practitioners in early years settings. Many of you will also be parents. What are the specific things that we can do to support a

The benefits of partnerships between parents/carers and practitioners.

Parents and carers	Practitioners	Young learners
Feel valued and respected by education professionals – maybe for the first time.	Understand better the background and cultural life of the young-learners in their setting. They can draw on this developed understanding to enhance the educational experience for all young-learners.	Feel valued and respected as individuals and feel as though the setting takes account of their background.
Are involved in their children's learning of mathematics and can develop their own mathematical understandings alongside their child.		Feels secure moving between home environments and the setting.
Can share information about their child. Can jointly celebrate successes and overcome challenges.	Can help children develop a sense of their own identity and belonging both in the setting and in the wider world.	Can transfer learning between experiences in and outside the setting.
Feel that their family and cultural background is respected and drawn on to enhance mathematical learning.	Can benefit from parents/carers knowledge, skills and expertise.	Can draw on contexts they understand from outside school to develop their mathematical understandings.
Feel comfortable in visiting an educational setting and talking to educational professionals.	Can provide a more emotionally secure environment for the children (and parents/carers and practitioners)	Benefit from the expertise of all the adults that support them in their learning.
Feel comfortable talking about mathematics.		
Understand more about the process of learning mathematics and can use this developing understanding to better support their child.		
Have an increased confidence in their own parenting skills.		

young learner in developing their understanding of mathematics in partnership? Firstly, as a parent, or in my case, as a grandparent, we could:

* Ask the practitioners in the setting the sorts of activities I can carry on at home which will support the mathematical learning they have been doing in school. Many schools use reading diaries to carry on discussions about the young-learners developing understanding of reading. Develop these sorts of discussions around mathematics.

* Whenever you are shopping, or cooking, or constructing something, or gardening, any activity that involves some mathematics, talk to your child about the activity. Ask them questions about what they notice and share your own observations

* Notice shapes, numbers, patterns in the environment and talk about them. Listen carefully to your child as they talk about what they notice and share the correct mathematical vocabulary with them. Share this learning with the child's practitioners in the setting.

* Play games and work at puzzles with your child. Build railway tracks, build towers and all the time talk and discuss what you notice. Talk about your plans for the track or the tower. Solve problems together.

* Talk to the practitioners in the setting about the types of resources they are using. If possible, get hold of similar resources to use at home.

* Look at the curriculum documents for the setting your child attends. They might give you ideas of activities you can try at home.

* What about practitioners? What might you be doing, as a practitioner, if you are working in partnership with parents and carers?

* Sharing information about the curriculum in as many ways as you can. This might be through a notice-board that parents and carers have to pass every day to let them know what mathematical activities are taking place that day. This might include photographs of the children working on mathematics.

* Send information home about the type of mathematical activities that children have been engaged in. Create a mathematics diary with suggestions of activities in it which parents and carers can comment in.

* Have discussions with parents and carers about the types of things that excite and motivate their child outside the setting. Draw on this enthusiasm to enrich the mathematical experiences in the setting. It may be that parents and carers can support you in the setting.

* Invite parents and carers into the setting to work on mathematics as a cultural experience. Cooking, sharing nursery rhymes, creating patterns.

I work with many teachers who work in international schools around the world. Their children come from a wide range of backgrounds and there are many different traditions and languages in any one classroom. In many of these classrooms there is an annual event, which one group of parents organise, that aims to share the culture and traditions of one of the nationalities within the classroom. This becomes a huge celebration. The children learn to cook the food, learn to recreate the cultural designs, explore cultural artefacts, engage in dancing and games and story-telling. In this way diversity is celebrated and seen as enhancing all our experience. Of course, most classrooms, in most schools around the world, could engage in this sort of event.

A partnership approach to assessment

One of the main differences between learning inside and outside a setting is that practitioners in a setting are held responsible by external agencies for the development of the learners in their setting. They measure this development and report on it, sometimes to parents and carers and sometimes to external agencies such as government inspectors. These assessments are much more effective if they are also seen as a partnership activity. This section draws heavily on the *Statutory Framework for the Early Years Foundation Stage* published by the Department for Education in England so that both practitioners and parents/carers are aware of the requirements placed on early years settings by government.

The framework reminds us that assessment is not purely to meet external demands but is a way of enabling all those who are interested in a child's developing understanding of mathematics to notice how this understanding is developing over time and supporting us in making decisions about the types of activities we might offer which will broaden this understanding. The framework notes that, "In their interactions with children, practitioners should respond to their own day-to-day observations about children's progress and observations that parents and carers share." This revisits the points made in the previous section of the importance of two-way communication between parents, carers and practitioners.

This type of assessment, often called formative assessment, is far removed from testing our children to check that they have certain skills or have retained particular pieces of knowledge. Formative assessment takes place all day every day and it is important that practitioners note these important observations to share with parents and carers. I remember receiving a report from my grandson's nursery with photographs of him building with magnetic shapes. The practitioner was delighted that he was using mathematical language whilst engaged in this activity. Grandad was delighted that the hours of play with the same resources at home was reflected in developing understanding showing itself in the nursery setting.

In England there is a national progress review between the ages of two and three and parents can expect to receive a summary of their child's development across the key areas. The best practice I have experienced integrates the areas of learning from the EYFS and provides photographs of the young learners engaged in an activity with a commentary linked to the Early Learning Goals. An example might be as follows. This is taken from my grandson's first report, sent electronically to the family when he was three years old. There is a photograph of my grandson playing a game where he is placing frogs on lily-pads. The photograph is annotated:

> **Notes**: During group time we practiced our counting skills and then matching to the correct numeral. We had five frogs sat on five longs. Each frog had a quantity of spots on their tummy that the children had to count and match them to the correct numeral on a lily-pad in the pond. The children did really well with their counting skills and the numeral recognition is really improving. For the children that required more challenge we introduced rolling a dice, counting out the corresponding number of frogs from a basket and matching them to the correct numeral on the lily pad.

There is more text which explains which areas of the Early Learning Goals are explored through this activity:

Aspects contributed to by this experience:

* Counts out up to six objects from a larger group. (Numbers: 40–60 months)
* Counts up to three or four objects by saying one number name for each item. (Numbers: 40–60 months)
* Recognise some numerals of personal significance. (Numbers: 40–60 months)
* Recognises numerals 1 to 5. (Numbers: 40–60 months)
* Selects the correct numeral to represent 1 to 5, then 1 to 10 objects. (Numbers: 40–60 months)

There were several such short commentaries in this report which gave the family a clear idea of his current mathematical understandings and offered ways to develop this understanding. It was suggested that we play a similar game at home using dice. As the report was sent electronically it was easy for mum and dad to share the report with other members of the family with caring roles.

At this stage any specific learning needs can be discussed with parents and carers to ensure that appropriate support is in place for all learners. This is also an ideal opportunity to discuss with parents and carers how learning can be developed at home, perhaps through an open event at which parents and carers engage in mathematical activity with their children and with the practitioners in the setting.

In addition to such formative assessment there is a more formal assessment when a child reaches five. This is, in part, to support the transition to Year 1. At this stage an Early

Years Foundation Stage (EYFS) profile is completed for each child. The framework states that this profile should provide, "parents and carers, practitioners and teachers with a well-rounded picture of a child's knowledge, understanding and abilities, their progress against expected levels, and their readiness for Year 1".

It is at this stage that judgements are made against the 'expected levels' of development. For me, this jars with the theme of each child as a unique individual and the statement which appears on every page of *Development Matters* (Early Education, 2012), "Children develop at their own rates, and in their own ways. The development statements and their order should not be taken as necessary steps for individual children. They should not be used as checklists."

However, if this assessment is carried out sensitively it can be used to support an important conversation between parents and carers and the early years practitioners and between early years practitioners and the teacher who is taking over responsibility for the mathematical development of the child the following year. Exemplification material is available in the *Early Years Foundation Stage Profile: 2017 Handbook* (Standards & Testing Agency, 2016). This restates the aims of mathematical activities in the Early Years which should provide children with opportunities to:

- practise and improve their skills in counting numbers, calculating simple addition and subtraction problems
- describe shapes, spaces, and measures

and describes both the Early Learning Goals in mathematics and describes what you might observe in children who are "exceeding" what might be "expected" at age five.

Descriptors for exceeding ELG in mathematics.

Early learning goal	Descriptors for children 'exceeding' goals
Goal 11. **Numbers**: children count reliably with numbers from 1 to 20, place them in order and say which number is one more or one less than a given number. Using quantities and objects, they add and subtract 2 single-digit numbers and count on or back to find the answer. They solve problems, including doubling, halving and sharing.	Children estimate a number of objects and check quantities by counting up to 20. They solve practical problems that involve combining groups of 2, 5 or 10, or sharing into equal groups.
Goal 12. **Shape, space and measures**: children use everyday language to talk about size, weight, capacity, position, distance, time and money to compare quantities and objects and to solve problems. They recognise, create and describe patterns. They explore characteristics of everyday objects and shapes and use mathematical language to describe them.	Children estimate, measure, weigh and compare and order objects and talk about properties, position and time.

We will look at this in more detail in the next chapter, which discusses the transition between an early years setting and the primary school. Let us finish this chapter with an image of an early years setting which is working on partnership with parents and carers well.

How do I know things are going well?

In the edition of *Nursery World* from November 2016, Jane Drake offers advice on how settings can ensure they are working effectively with parents and practitioners. To return to the opening of this chapter, where we discussed what would make an ideal setting for all children, I have used her suggestions to create an image of an early years setting in which I would feel secure that all children would learn and develop in their mathematical understandings. This may help practitioners reflect on how the setting in which they work marches the best settings out there. It may also help those of you who are parents when you look for a setting that will support your child effectively.

> As I arrive at the setting with my grandson we spend some time watching the slide-show on the screen just outside the setting. A loop of photographs has been set up and they have just added images from the visit to the airport last week. Unusually for my grandson he actually talks about what he did at school, explaining how the seats on an aircraft are arranged and where the "crew" sit. There is a poster next to the screen from the airport which show all the areas that the children visited. This has been annotated by one of the practitioners. It is clear that these annotations have been completed after a discussion with the children.

> We pass the noticeboard by the door to the setting and I glance at it to check the times of the holiday breaks and to see what the main themes for learning are going to be for the next term. Another parent, the mum of a young polish boy that my grandson loves playing with, picks up a leaflet about supporting reading. This is available in Polish and she tells me that her mum really likes reading the leaflets, so she can "teach reading" to her grandchildren. I also notice that there is a workshop next week to talk to parents and carers about the new magnetic construction materials that the setting has just purchased. I make a note of the name of the resources, a great idea for a Christmas present!

> As always, I am inspired by the activities set up in the outside area – it looks like the sand and water play will be fun today. I am delighted to see many different types of containers by the water tray.

Figure 1.10 Cuisenaire® rods in a truck

As we make our way through the door of the setting one of the practitioners smiles and tells me that they enjoyed finding out that my grandson had enjoyed packing Cuisenaire® rods into lorries to make "bales of hay". They had let him go up into the primary school classes who use Cuisenaire® rods to borrow some and have put in an order for their own sets.

The practitioner finds out that I visit every Friday and asks if we can plan a time for me to come in and talk to all the practitioners about early years mathematics as she hadn't realised that this was my background. We sort this out quickly. When I talk to my daughter later in the day she tells me how "Mrs G", as my grandson calls his teacher, has always been open and excited about my grandson's interests. She has also been trying to get his dad to go into the setting and cook with the children ever since she found out he was a chef. She has contacted them on a couple of occasions when she has noticed something worrying my grandson.

My daughter and son-in-law meet "Mrs G" once a term. These have been organised on a Tuesday afternoon as this is the only day off that they share. The setting is organised so that the key-worker can have time during the day to meet parents and carers in a more structured way. My daughter really values these meetings as they give her space to talk about any worries she has and to learn lots about what goes on in the setting during the day. As with many children, my grandson is not always very forthcoming about what he has been working on during the day once he gets home. She says that she always comes home from these meetings feeling excited about what my grandson is achieving and with lots of great ideas for things to work on at home. She was offered a meeting at home with the key-worker but says that she would much rather go into the setting as she can see all the resources that are available.

The setting have just started a new partnership-project. Parents can borrow digital cameras to take photographs of their children engaged in activity at home or outside to create a "home-report". The key-worker will use these images to supplement the early years profile that she is putting together so that this profile acknowledges all the learning experiences whether they take place in the setting or at home.

My grandson sees a friend and goes straight over to one of the indoor stations to carry on making "the biggest factory in the world". The construction has been left from yesterday so that he can carry on with this construction which he was telling me about, very proudly, last night.

Yes, this is an ideal – and, yes, I understand that very real constraints such as time and money come into play as soon as we have to make decisions about how we will organize the learning experiences for the young-learners in our care. But, everything I have described above I have seen in settings I have visited.

In a nutshell

1. Early years practitioners should see and treat parents and carers as partners in the education of the child drawing on the knowledge that they have of the child's development and interests.

2. Two-way communication, through a key-worker for each child, with parents and carers is vital.

3. All assessments of a child's learning and progress should be shared with parents and carers.

References

Aistear. *Building partnerships between parents and practitioners.* Available at http://www.ncca.biz/Aistear/pdfs/Guidelines_ENG/Practitioners_ENG.pdf (accessed 13 March 2018).

Department for Education and Science (DES) (1975) *A language for Life: The Bullock Report.* London: Department for Education.

Department for Education (DfE) (2017) *Statutory framework for the early years foundation stage: Setting the standards for learning, development and care for children from birth to five.* London: HMSO.

Drake, J. (2006) Working with parents to support children's learning *Nursery World* 15 November 2006. Available at https://www.nurseryworld.co.uk/nursery-world/news/1080052/working-with-parents-to-support-childrens-learning (accessed 15 March 2018).

Early Education (2012) *Development matters in the Early Years Foundation Stage (EYFS)*. London: The British Association for Early Childhood Education.

Standards & Testing Agency (2016) *Early years foundation stage profile: 2017 handbook*. Available at https://www.foundationyears.org.uk/files/2017/02/2017_EYFSP_handbook_v1.1.pdf (accessed 16 March 2018).

The Early Years Foundation Stage. *Effective practice: Parents as partners* Available at http://www.keap.org.uk/documents/eyfs_eff_prac_parent_partner.pdf (accessed 13 March 2018).

4 Preparing for 'big school'

In a world of social media, the first day of 'school' is often accompanied by the putting on of a new uniform, and has become a widely shared event. Photographs of proud parents with occasionally underwhelmed offspring in this strange new outfit are shared across social media platforms. But behind this image, what has been done to prepare the young learner for this transition in their education and what can parents and practitioners do to make this transition as seamless as possible. Maybe the first piece of advice should be, "don't make such a big deal of it". But clearly, there is more to it than that.

My aim in this chapter gives advice to practitioners working in early years settings as they prepare for the move into what is often a more formal primary education. This includes describing what primary teachers in England might normally expect a child beginning primary school to be able to do, know and understand. As in previous chapters, this expectation is compared to expectations in the PYP and New Zealand curricula as a way of opening the discussion about the first stages of mathematics in primary education.

The chapter moves on to explore how teaching and learning might be organised differently in the first stages of primary education to a kindergarten or early years setting. Finally, we explore how parents and carers might support their child make a comfortable transition into primary school, such as possible questions to ask when they meet the teacher for the first time and what to look for in the new classroom as they look around with their child. But before any of this I want to discuss a bigger question. When is the best time for children to begin their formal education?

When are children ready for primary school?

Currently, in England most children start school in the September following their fourth birthday. They will join a reception class as many early years settings are called. Of course, many children will have spent time in other settings before this, sometimes nursery schools and sometimes at child-minders. Many of these settings call themselves "pre-school". As I wrote earlier, I worry a little about this phrase as it suggests that the purpose of this setting is to prepare children for 'school'. These early years settings are important places of education themselves, in the sense that they are places where young children are learning.

A report published by the National Foundation for Educational Research (NFER) in 2002 points out that the UK is out of step with many other countries in starting formal education this early. A table included in the research paper compares the age that children start school in a range of European countries.

School starting age in Europe.

Starting age (in years)	Countries
4	Northern Ireland
5	England, Malta, Netherlands, Scotland, Wales
6	Austria, Belgium, Cyprus, Czech Republic, France, Germany, Greece, Hungary, Iceland, Republic of Ireland, Italy, Liechtenstein, Lithuania, Luxembourg, Norway, Portugal, Slovakia, Spain
7	Bulgaria, Estonia, Denmark, Finland, Latvia, Poland, Romania, Sweden

The most common age for starting school around the world is six and children in the countries who regularly perform well in international studies (including Singapore and China) do not start school until a year later than their counterparts in the UK. I share this information not to criticise policy in early years settings in the UK but, once more, to try to reduce the pressure that early years practitioners say they feel, to teach reading, writing and mathematical skills. The NFER report (Sharp, 2002, p. 16) states:

> The evidence consistently shows that this early advantage [from teaching these skills early] is not sustained in the long term. Children who are taught these skills up to three years later seem to acquire them rapidly, and thereafter perform as well as or better than children with an early start.

The author goes on to say that young children learn most effectively when they have "opportunities to socialise, make their own choices and take responsibility for their own learning". This suggests to me that one of the most important roles early years practitioners can play is to support young learners in becoming social learners and in taking responsibility for their own learning and for making good choices that will support their learning. In this way, we will be teaching children how to learn, a skill that they can take with them into primary classrooms and beyond.

What are the expectations?

Chapter 1 dealt in depth with the expectations on the types of mathematical skills and knowledge children would be taught in the early years of schooling. And knowing the expectations at the end of the first year in primary school can help early years practitioners in planning appropriate activities to support the transition. But, do remember, this does not mean that the children should meet the expectations before they start primary school. And, remember, from above, the evidence does not suggest there is any advantage to be gained in teaching these skills early. I have adapted the English National Curriculum so that it reads as a narrative, as in the Early Learning Goals, rather than a set of bullet points.

I leave you to make your own judgements about how to use this table to prepare young learners for the move into primary school. My interpretation is that if I have been providing lots of practical activities that involve counting and adding objects or taking objects away; if I have been encouraging children to make their own marks to record these activities; and if there are lots of different representations of the number system in the setting, my learners will be well prepared for primary school.

Similarly, if children have been comparing objects using non-standard measures, measuring and weighing, using coins and notes in the role-play area, if I have been referring to the time on the analogue and digital clocks in the setting and if we have played games involving sequencing time they will be well prepared for their developing learning in measuring.

Finally, if we have been noticing, naming and talking about two-dimensional and three-dimensional shapes and noticing, creating and describing patterns, the children should be able to access the learning they will encounter around shape, space and algebra.

I also chose to include early data handling and statistical enquiries. Not because I have to, not because it is in the curriculum, but because it is an engaging and motivating thing to do. It sets numbers in a real context and it provides great opportunities for discussion. These are the areas that are covered in section 2 with a range of activities for you to engage in with the younglearners in your setting.

Organising teaching and learning over the transition

In July 2007, Sir Peter Williams was asked by the UK Government to undertake a comprehensive review into mathematics teaching in early years settings and primary schools (Williams, 2008). Although a change of government meant that most of the recommendations were not fully implemented this offers us the clearest recent advice based on research evidence and an extensive programme of visits to settings and classrooms.

Expectations of learning at the end of Stage 1.

Area	Early Learning Goals	End of Year 1 expectations	PYP Stage 1 expectations	New Zealand Mathematics Stage 1 expectations
Number	Children count reliably with numbers from 1 to 20, place them in order and say which number is one more or one less than a given number. Using quantities and objects, they add and subtract two single-digit numbers and count on or back to find the answer. They solve problems, including doubling, halving and sharing.	Children should read and write numbers from 1 to 20 in numerals and words and count forwards and backwards up to 100. They should recognise and write the numerals to 100 and be able to count in 1s, 2s, 5s and 10s. They will find 1 more and 1 less than a given number and represent numbers using objects and pictorial representations including the number line. They will use the language of: equal to, more than, less than (fewer), most, least. They know and write addition and subtraction facts to 20 and solve one-step addition, subtraction and multiplication problems using concrete objects and pictorial representations They should recognise ½ and ¼ of shapes and quantities.	Children will understand that numbers are used for many different purposes in the real world. They will develop an understanding of one-to-one correspondence and conservation of number, and be able to count and use number words and numerals to represent quantities	Children will use a range of counting, grouping, and equal-sharing strategies with whole numbers and fractions. They will know the forward and backward counting sequences of whole numbers to 100. They will also know groupings with five, within ten, and with ten.
Shape and space	Children explore characteristics of everyday objects and shapes and use mathematical language to describe them.	Children should recognise common 2-D and 3-D shapes and describe position, direction and movement including whole, half, quarter and three=quarter turns.	Children will understand that shapes have characteristics that can be described and compared. They will understand and use common language to describe paths, regions and boundaries of their immediate environment.	Children will sort objects by their appearance. They will give and follow instructions for movement that involve distances, directions, and half or quarter turns and describe their position relative to a person or object. They will communicate and record the results of translations, reflections, and rotations on plane shapes.

continued

Continued

Measures	Children use everyday language to talk about size, weight, capacity, position, distance, time and money to compare quantities and objects and to solve problems.	Children should compare, describe and solve practical problems for lengths, weights, capacities and time. They should recognise the values of different coins and sequence events chronologically. They should tell the time to the hour and half-hour.	Children will develop an understanding of how measurement involves the comparison of objects and sequencing of events. They will be able to identify, compare and describe attributes of real objects as well as describe and sequence familiar events in their daily routine.	Children will order and compare objects or events by length, area, volume and capacity, weight (mass), turn (angle), temperature, and time by direct comparison and/or counting whole numbers of units.
Algebra	Children recognise, create and describe patterns	Children recognise and create repeating patterns with objects and shapes.	Children will understand that patterns and sequences occur in everyday situations. They will be able to identify, describe, extend and create patterns in various ways.	Children will generalise that the next counting number gives the result of adding one object to a set and that counting the number of objects in a set tells how many. They will create and continue sequential patterns.
Data handling		Does not appear in English curriculum	Children will develop an understanding of how the collection and organisation of information helps to make sense of the world. They will sort, describe and label objects by attributes and represent information in graphs including pictographs and tally marks. The learners will discuss chance in daily events.	Children will conduct investigations using the statistical enquiry cycle: posing and answering questions gathering, sorting and counting, and displaying category data and discussing the results. They will interpret statements made by others from statistical investigations and probability activities and investigate situations that involve elements of chance, acknowledging and anticipating possible outcomes.

There was also a widespread consultation with teachers and practitioners. The focus of the report was not on the content of the curriculum but on pedagogy. It is because of this that we can draw on the report to explore what parents should expect to see in a primary classroom and what practitioners in early years settings might prepare children for.

The report notes the discontinuity in the language used between the Early Years Framework and the National Curriculum. I have already mentioned the change in emphasis, moving from every learner being unique and learning at their own pace to the assumption that all learners will "progress at approximately the same pace". It also describes how the Early Years Foundation Stage describes mathematical experiences under the heading, 'Problem solving and numeracy', with seven of the twelve Early Learning Goals focused around number. This suggests a mathematical curriculum which is connected and broad and which is focused on problem solving. The Williams review suggests that this view of mathematics should continue into the first stages of primary school in order to offer learners a continuous and coherent mathematical experience.

This continuity of experience should also act as a bridge between the pedagogical approaches in the early years and primary school. The report notes that practitioners talked about an abrupt transition between play-based learning focused on mathematical problem solving in the early years and a more formal approach in the first years of primary school. The report suggests that,

> A case can be advanced for slightly more emphasis in Reception and Year 1 on play-based learning, with a focus on extending the use of more structured activity to prepare children for this transition.
>
> (Williams, 2008, p. 63)

This suggests that an aspect of effective transition would be good communication between the early years setting and the primary classroom so that such continuity can be ensured. The report notes that whilst many schools developed confidence with numbers through starting with counting activities and other practical activities before developing these ideas in more abstract ways, other schools chose to stress concrete, abstract and algebraic aspects of mathematics at an early stage using resources such as Cuisenaire® rods. Both of these approaches were seen to be successful. This suggests that it is the skills and understandings of the teachers and practitioners that is important and not simply the chosen pedagogical approach. Whatever the approach, the key for effective transition is that the early years setting and the primary classroom share resources and share professional development so that teachers and practitioners are equally skilled in the chosen approach.

An area that we have discussed in previous chapters is developing young learners' skills in recording mathematics, whether this is through symbols, images or numerals. As they move through the primary school they will learn that this recording needs to become more precise as mathematics is about precision. This is not to suggest that there should be a rapid change in the expectation on children's recording. On the contrary, children's own mark-making should be encouraged into primary school and gradually, through careful and sensitive modelling and teaching children will become skilled in using a wide-range of diagrams, tables and graphs to record their mathematical thinking. These written skills will be developed alongside the children's oral skills as they explain ever more complex mathematical ideas.

Finally, the report raises a concern that early years settings and primary schools do not emphasise the development of young-learners' positive attitudes to mathematics. This can be a result of practitioners in early years settings not being overt about the mathematical activity present in the setting. Rather than celebrating the mathematical skills on view, they will say to me, "that was a fantastic activity, the children didn't even know they were doing mathematics". How much better it would be if children moved into primary school aware of themselves as successful learners of mathematics.

A report written for the New Zealand government by Hilary Fabian and Aline-Wendy Dunlop (Fabian and Dunlop, 2006) arrived at similar conclusions. Their report, *Outcomes of Good Practice in Transition Processes for Children Entering Primary School* identified three areas for practitioners and teachers to focus on.

Firstly, activities that support a **continuity in the learning experience** across the transition. These activities would include workshops for parents, carers and children which would introduce them to the types of learning experiences that will be available once the children start school. This means that the first day at school is actually just another visit to a familiar space. Similarly, there is no hard transition to new expectations in terms of children's participation in a learning experience or sharp shift in teaching strategies. This sort of continuity can also be supported by using play-based activities that children are familiar with in the early years setting and even continuing to explore activities that have been started in the early years setting. Ideally children who are already within the school can act as mentors or 'buddies' to the new arrivals. This has huge benefits for the new starters and for the children acting as mentors. Finally, and perhaps most importantly it is vital that the staff in the new setting make the most of communication between the two sets of staff to become aware of each child's individual learning needs before they transfer. In this way each child remains a unique individual.

Secondly, the early years setting and the school should find ways to support **continuity in social and emotional well-being** across the transition. This continuity is vital to ensure that positive relationships parents and carers have formed with early years practitioners are maintained as their children move into primary school. A child that feels safe and emotionally secure is much better placed to learn effectively and is more likely to participate and engage fully in the learning experiences on offer. If a child feels emotionally secure in the classroom they will become confident in their own abilities as learners and are more likely to take responsibility for their learning. This continuity can be supported by ensuring there is some form of continuity in the day-to-day classroom routines and the environment of the classroom feels familiar to the learners. In some ways it should reflect the early-years setting from which they have come. An initial activity which involves learners talking about things that are important to them, maybe a particular toy that they play with, or an important space at home can make them feel as though their own needs are valued in the new classroom and can begin to create a community of learners within the new classroom.

There will be new routines and a new language of school for children to get used to. Teachers can support children in becoming used to the new culture of the classroom by open discussions in circle time about the changes. New 'rules' can be negotiated. An activity which asks children to create 'golden rules' for the classroom including their expectations of their teachers can be a successful way to introduce new rules. Classrooms who have tried this activity always report that the children are great at coming up with the type of rules which might have been expected, such as, listening carefully, sharing, completing tasks, asking for help if they need it and being polite and respectful. Interestingly, teachers also report that children place these expectations on their teachers too.

Another important factor for developing secure space for children to learn is ensuring that the support of friends is available. I still remember the ritual of 'thumbs up and thumbs down' when my children attended primary school. Whilst the children queued in the playground before going into school they would pick out someone who they hoped would be their friend for the day. A thumbs-up would be affirmation, but a thumbs-down could lead to tears. This was only sorted out when the teacher overtly dealt with the issue, again, through circle time.

Fabian and Dunlop also remind us that **communication across the transition** is key to ensuring the children make the best start they possibly can. This allows the move into primary school to be much less mysterious. Perhaps, as parents, we can support teachers in demystifying the transition by presenting the move as a completely normal and usual thing to happen. Let's stop taking special photos and posting these on social media. Let's treat the first day in school as just another day. School can help by being very clear in their communication about the transition. If the parents and carers know exactly what is likely to happen in the new classroom they can share this information with their children and be confident about the transition. If the parents and carers are confident about the transition this will be passed on to the children.

Questions to ask at transition

This final section aims to support parents and carers who are visiting the primary school which their child will be moving into. I hope it will be useful to those of you that teach in a primary school as you can reflect on how you might answer these questions if a parent or a carer asked them of you. Finally, readers who are early years practitioners can use these questions to explore how well they know the classrooms into which the young learners in their care will be moving. These questions draw on the discussion above:

- How do you provide for children's individual learning needs? How do you know what these needs might be?

- How will you know what my child's accomplishments in mathematics are?

- How do you know the sort of mathematical experiences that my child has enjoyed previously?

- How have you worked with the early years setting to support the continuity of learning experiences in mathematics?

- Will my child be expected to be actively involved in mathematical-problem solving? Can you give me an example of what this might look like?

- How do you continue to develop positive attitudes to mathematics? Can you give me an example of what this might look like in the classroom?

- How do you make sure that mathematical learning is included across the curriculum?

- How do you use the role-play area to support the learning of mathematics?

- How do you use the outdoor environment to support the learning of mathematics?

- What resources do you use to support the learning of mathematics?

- How do you remain up-to-date with current developments in learning and teaching mathematics?

- What recent changes have you made to your classroom practice in teaching mathematics?

In a nutshell

1. The importance of communication between an early years setting and the primary classroom into which young learners will move to ensure continuity and coherence in terms of:

   ○ Pedagogical approaches based on play, activity and problem solving including shared professional development on approaches to learning and teaching mathematics

   ○ Children's developing recording of their thinking including mark-making

   ○ Developing positive attitudes towards mathematics

   ○ Social and emotional well-being

2. The importance of communication between early years settings and the primary classroom with parents and carers to demystify the transition. Confident parents and carers leads to confident children.

References

Fabian and Dunlop (2006) *Continuity of learning*. Available at http://www.ero.govt.nz/assets/Uploads/ERO-Continuity-of-Learning-Brochure-A4-FINAL.pdf (accessed 22 March 2018).

NCETM (2016) *The essence of teaching for mastery*. Available at https://www.ncetm.org.uk/files/37086535/The+Essence+of+Maths+Teaching+for+Mastery+june+2016.pdf (accessed March 21st 2018).

Sharp, C. (2002) School starting age: European policy and recent research. NFER. Available at https://www.nfer.ac.uk/publications/44414/44414.pdf (accessed 21 March 2018).

Williams, P. (2008) Independent review of mathematics teaching in early years settings and primary schools. Department for children, schools and families. Available at http://dera.ioe.ac.uk/8365/7/Williams%20Mathematics_Redacted.pdf (accessed 20 March 2018).

2

Activities to develop confident young mathematicians

Introduction

The first section of the book described how children come to an understanding of mathematics in the first five years of their lives. We discussed how we might describe mathematics and mathematical thinking and outlined a range of expectations of the sorts of mathematical skills and understandings that young children will develop. This section also covers mathematics from birth to five. It offers a range of practical activities with suggestions for adult–child interactions which will support the children in their mathematical development. It will also explain why the particular activities are mathematical and how these activities lead into the sorts of skills that might be expected when the children start school.

The activities are organized in six key areas. These do not directly match the Early Years Foundation Stage guidance as I have chosen to separate shape, space and measures and to include algebra (through describing and creating patterns) and data handling. These areas both contribute to the development of the understanding of number and are discrete areas in both the Primary Years Programme (PYP) of the International Baccalaureate (IB) and other internationally recognised curricula. So, you will find activities in the following areas:

- Number: counting and ordering
- Number: calculating
- Shape and space
- Measurement
- Algebra
- Data handling

The table below uses the prefix 'mainly' to acknowledge that mathematics is viewed as a connected subject and that no activity can be seen as solely contributing to one area of mathematics. There are a total of 60 activities and each is presented in the same way. Firstly, there is information on how to set up the activity including the resources that you will need. Where possible I have used resources that can be found in any classroom or home. This is to suggest that it is not always necessary to have specialist resources to learn mathematics as mathematics exists all around us in the everyday objects that we encounter.

Next there is a description of 'What to do' as you explore the activity with the children followed by the questions you could use to move children's learning forward. This is labelled 'What to ask'. The left-hand page of each activity also lists the keywords or phrases that you should focus on during the activity. All of these words are included in the glossary at the end of the book. Finally, there is discussion about how you can develop this activity.

The facing page for each activity describes the mathematical understandings that children will be developing through engaging in the activity and links this to the Early Learning Goals and the development stages which were outlined in Section 1. This page also outlines the problem solving skills that are being developed using criteria developed by Sue Gifford in her article available from the NRich website. These are:

- Getting to grips with the problem
- connecting to previous experience
- planning
- considering alternatives
- monitoring progress
- evaluating solutions

This facing page also outlines how to encourage discussion and the links you can make to children's experiences outside the setting. In addition to this, possible misconceptions or difficulties which you may observe are described and the subject knowledge you will need to fully develop the activity is detailed. The final area dealt with is that of personal and emotional development. Drawing on the Early Learning Goal:

Making relationships
Children play co-operatively, taking turns with others. They take account of one another's ideas about how to organize their activity. They show sensitivity to others' needs and feelings, and form positive relationships with adults and other children.

Self-confidence and self-awareness
Children are confident to try new activities, and say why they like some activities more than others. They are confident to speak in a familiar group, will talk about their ideas, and will choose the resources they need for their chosen activity

Managing feelings and behaviour

Children talk about how they and others show feelings, talk about their own and others' behaviour, and its consequences, and know that some behaviour is unacceptable. They work as part of a group or class, and understand and follow the rules. They adjust their behaviour to different situations, and take changes of routine in their stride.

Practitioners can see how they can use the activity to support children's personal social and emotional development.

References

Gifford, S. *Mathematical problem solving in the early years: Developing opportunities, strategies and confidence.* Available at https://nrich.maths.org/12166 (accessed 27 March 2018).

◼ Activities

5 Mainly number
Counting and ordering

The activities in this section develop the following mathematical skills:

Age range	What a child is learning
Birth–11 months	Notices changes in number of objects/images or sounds in group of up to 3.
8–20 months	Develops an awareness of number names through their enjoyment of action rhymes and songs that relate to their experience of numbers.
16–26 months	Says some counting words randomly.
22–36 months	Recites some number names in sequence.
	Creates and experiments with symbols and marks representing ideas of number.
30–50 months	Uses some number names and number language spontaneously.
	Uses some number names accurately in play.
	Recites numbers in order to 10.
	Beginning to represent numbers using fingers, marks on paper or pictures.
	Shows curiosity about numbers by offering comments or asking questions.
	Shows an interest in numerals in the environment.
	Shows an interest in representing numbers.
	Realises not only objects, but anything can be counted, including steps, claps or jumps.
40–60+ months	Recognise some numerals of personal significance.
	Recognises numerals 1 to 5.
	Counts up to three or four objects by saying one number name for each item.
	Counts actions or objects which cannot be moved.
	Counts objects to 10, and beginning to count beyond 10.
	Counts out up to six objects from a larger group.
	Selects the correct numeral to represent 1 to 5, then 1 to 10 objects.
	Counts an irregular arrangement of up to ten objects.
	Estimates how many objects they can see and checks by counting them.
	Records, using marks that they can interpret and explain.

Remember, children develop at their own rates, and in their own ways. These statements and their order should not be taken as necessary steps or checklists for individual children.

By the end of Year 1 children should:

> count reliably with numbers from 1 to 20, place them in order and say which number is one more or one less than a given number. Using quantities and objects, add and subtract two single-digit numbers and count on or back to find the answer.... . solve problems, including doubling, halving and sharing.

Routine activities

There are many opportunities for counting and ordering in the routines of the school day, from taking the register, to collecting dinner money, to organising groups of learners. These should mainly be opportunities for you to model counting so that children hear the 'counting numbers' regularly. Birthdays are good ways of recognising numbers of personal significance, including birthdays of siblings and parents or carers (and practitioners!)

Regularly use number rhymes. They are a great way to end the day. You could ask parents or carers who arrive early to collect their children to share rhymes they know.

Activity 1: Blast off

Setting up the activity: This activity can take place inside and outside.

Inside: Use building blocks, or magnetic construction materials. Cut out a series of images of space ships and rockets, real and imaginary. If possible have a tablet available with video of a rocket taking off. Many of these videos include a "count-down". Find story books which include a rocket taking off and a count-down.

Outside: Use large building blocks or construction materials. Alternatively, you can use large boxes or other scrap materials to create larger rockets.

What to do:
Read the story or watch the video. Read together and join in the count-down.

Use the modelling materials to build a range of rockets. As you build the rockets talk about the shapes that you are using and compare the sizes of the rockets.

When the rockets are built take it in turns to count-down to blast-off.

Ask the whole class to come over to look at the rockets.

Repeat the count-down as a whole class.

Recording:
Use white-boards to record the count-down in any way the children choose.

What to ask:
What shape will you need to use next?
Is that rocket big enough for you to get in?
Which is the tallest rocket?
What are you going to add next?
Is that finished?

Words to use:
Square, triangle, rectangle – talking about the 2-dimensional faces of the shapes you are using.
Cuboid, pyramid – talking about the 3-dimensional building blocks.
Taller, taller, tallest – when comparing the space ships.
Wide, wider, widest – when comparing the space ships.
Small, smaller, smallest – when comparing the space ships.
Cardinal numbers from 1–10. (One, two, three, four and so on.)

To develop the activity:
Build space-ships so that particular toys can fit in them. These may be dolls or other toy people or toy animals or the child's favourite toy.

If you are using building blocks you can compare the sizes of the space-ships by counting how many blocks high they are.

When counting down take it in turns to say numbers. For example, the practitioner counts down the even numbers and the children the odd or vice-versa. Alternatively clap alternate numbers. So:

10, clap, 8, clap, 6, clap, 4, clap, 2, clap – BLAST OFF!

Mathematical development

Age range	What a child is learning
Birth–11 months	Notices changes in number of objects/images or sounds in group of up to 3.
8–20 months	Develops an awareness of number names through their enjoyment of action rhymes and songs that relate to their experience of numbers.
16–26 months	Says some counting words randomly.
22–36 months	Recites some number names in sequence.
	Creates and experiments with symbols and marks representing ideas of number.
30–50 months	Uses some number names and number language spontaneously.
	Uses some number names accurately in play.
	Recites numbers in order to 10.
	Beginning to represent numbers using fingers, marks on paper or pictures.
	Shows curiosity about numbers by offering comments or asking questions.
	Shows an interest in numerals in the environment.
	Shows an interest in representing numbers.
	Realises not only objects, but anything can be counted, including steps, claps or jumps.
40–60+ months	Recognise some numerals of personal significance.
	Recognises numerals 1 to 5.
	Counts up to three or four objects by saying one number name for each item.
	Counts actions or objects which cannot be moved.

Active learning
Building the rockets and discussing the design.
Chanting the count-down together.

Problem solving skills
Planning how to build a rocket suitable for a particular toy. Checking that the size is correct. Comparing rockets made by different groups.

Encouraging discussion
Encourage children to talk about the rockets they are making as they build them.

Links to prior experiences
Talk about other books or films that contain space-travel.
Talk about toys that have that are linked to space travel.

Possible misconceptions or difficulties
Omitting numbers from count.
Not understanding stable-order principle.

Subject knowledge for practitioners
Model accurate mathematical vocabulary for shapes when building rockets.
Model counting backwards.

Personal and emotional development
Planning activity together.
Speak about their ideas.
Confident to try new ideas.
Work as part of a group.

Activity 2: Aliens

Setting up the activity: This activity can take place inside and outside.
Inside: Use scrap materials or art materials. These should be available on the table. Cut out a series of images of aliens from magazines or the web. If possible have a tablet available with a video of aliens. Find story books which include stories of aliens.
Outside: Use large building blocks or other scrap materials to create 'life-size' aliens.

What to do:
Read the story or watch the video. Talk about the aliens. What do the children notice? Choose a story where the aliens do not all have 2 arms and 2 legs and 5 fingers and toes.

Use the modelling or art materials to make aliens. As you build the rockets talk about the sizes and shapes of the body parts of the aliens.

Create aliens with different numbers of legs and arms and fingers and toes.

As a group count the numbers of arms and legs and fingers and fingers and toes on the aliens.

Recording:
Use white-boards to record the numbers of limbs in any way the children choose.

What to ask:
What is the same/what is different about those two aliens?

Words to use:
Square, triangle, rectangle – talking about the 2-dimensional shapes when drawing the aliens.
Cuboid, pyramid – talking about the 3-dimensional building blocks if building aliens.
Tall, taller, tallest – when comparing the aliens.
Wide, wider, widest – when comparing the aliens.
Small, smaller, smallest – when comparing the aliens.
Most/fewest fingers – when comparing the aliens.
Cardinal numbers from 1–10.

To develop the activity:
Ask how many more/how many less when comparing the aliens.
Make an alien with a total of 8 limbs/15 digits/8 fingers.

Mathematical development

Age range	What a child is learning
Birth–11 months	Notices changes in number of objects/images or sounds in group of up to 3.
8–20 months	Develops an awareness of number names
16–26 months	Says some counting words randomly.
22–36 months	Recites some number names in sequence.
	Creates and experiments with symbols and marks representing ideas of number.
30–50 months	Uses some number names and number language spontaneously.
	Uses some number names accurately in play.
	Recites numbers in order to 10.
	Beginning to represent numbers using fingers, marks on paper or pictures.
	Shows curiosity about numbers by offering comments or asking questions.
	Shows an interest in numerals in the environment.
	Shows an interest in representing numbers.
40–60+ months	Recognise some numerals of personal significance.
	Recognises numerals 1 to 5.
	Counts up to three or four objects by saying one number name for each item.
	Counts actions or objects which cannot be moved.
	Counts objects to 10 and beginning to count beyond 10.
	Selects the correct numeral to represent 1 to 5, then 1 to 10 objects.
	Records, using marks that they can interpret and explain.

Active learning
Drawing or building aliens and talking about them.

Problem solving skills
Planning the sort of alien they will draw. Telling you how many fingers or toes they will draw. Talking about the aliens.

Encouraging discussion
Comparing the aliens – what is the same and what is different?

Links to prior experiences
Describing books they have read or films they have seen which include aliens.

Possible misconceptions or difficulties
Not counting accurately – count with the children to model the stable order principle.

Subject knowledge for practitioners
Model accurate mathematical vocabulary for shapes when drawing or creating the aliens.
Model counting accurately – touch the limbs as you count them.

Personal and emotional development
Planning activity together.
Speak about their ideas.
Being sensitive to others.
Confident to try new ideas.
Work as part of a group.

Activity 3: Fish race

Setting up the activity: Make at least five fish of different colours using tissue paper or other coloured paper. These should be about 30cm long by 15cm wide but should be different lengths and widths. You might need to test them to make sure that they can be 'flapped' along with a newspaper.

You need newspapers to use to flap the fish.

Create a grid at the finish so that the children can stand in order at the end

First – 1st	Second – 2nd	Third – 3rd	Fourth – 4th	Fifth – 5th

What to do:
Pick five children to play the game.
They play the game by flapping the fish along the floor from a start line to a finish line.
The winning fish is placed on the First place and so on.
Repeat several times.

Recording:
Children should record the results on a white-board in any way they wish.
Ask them to record which fish wins the most.

What to ask:
Who do you think is going to be first?
What position is yellow in?
Who is next to blue?
Do you think the longest/shortest fish will win?

Words to use:
The ordinal numbers – first, second, third, fourth, fifth.
Long/longest/short/shortest, thinnest/widest – when comparing the fish.

To develop the activity:
Use more fish.
Ask children to create their own fish to specific designs.
What strategies can children use to win?
What are the fewest flaps to get from the beginning to the end?

Mathematical development

Age range	What a child is learning
Birth–11 months	Notices changes in number of objects/images or sounds in group of up to 3.
8–20 months	Develops an awareness of number names through their enjoyment of action rhymes and songs that relate to their experience of numbers.
16–26 months	Says some counting words randomly.
22–36 months	Recites some number names in sequence. Creates and experiments with symbols and marks representing ideas of number.
30–50 months	Uses some number names and number language spontaneously. Uses some number names accurately in play. Beginning to represent numbers using fingers, marks on paper or pictures. Shows curiosity about numbers by offering comments or asking questions.
40–60+ months	Recognise some numerals of personal significance. Recognises numerals 1 to 5. Selects the correct numeral to represent 1 to 5, then 1 to 10 objects. Records, using marks that they can interpret and explain.

Active learning
Playing the flapping game.

Problem solving skills
Predicting which fish might win.
Coming up with a strategy for winning the game.
Designing a fish which will win the game.

Encouraging discussion
Create teams of children to play game who have to plan a strategy.
Talk about how to record the results.

Links to prior experiences
What other games do children play in which they have 'positions'?
What do they watch on the television where things are placed in order?

Possible misconceptions or difficulties
Mixing up cardinal and ordinal numbers – model the use of ordinal numbers with the pupils.
Continue in the morning when the children are queuing up in the morning for example.

Subject knowledge for practitioners
Ordinal numbers.

Personal and emotional development
Cooperating and taking turns.
Being sensitive to others.
Work as part of a group.
Adapt to change.

Activity 4: Horse race

Setting up the activity: Create a board for a horse race.

1	2	3	4	5	6

Use model horses or counters to act as horses. There also need to be a box of dice on the table. Alternatively play the game using a large grid on the floor, a large foam dice and children to be the 'horses'.

What to do:
The children take it in turns to pick a horse that they think will win.
They roll the dice. If they roll a three they move horse 3 and so on.
Take it in turns to roll the dice until one horse has won.
Repeat several times – predicting which horse they think will win each time and giving a reason why.

Recording:
Children should record which horses win the game in any way they wish.

What to ask:
Which horse is winning?
Who do you think will win? Why?

Words to use:
Model the accurate pronunciation of the numbers on the dice.

To develop the activity:
Count how many turns it takes to finish the game.
Describe the relative positions of the horses at the end of the game.

Mathematical development

Age range	What a child is learning
Birth–11 months	Notices changes in number of objects/images or sounds in group of up to 3.
8–20 months	Develops an awareness of number names through their enjoyment of action rhymes and songs that relate to their experience of numbers.
16–26 months	Says some counting words randomly.
22–36 months	Creates and experiments with symbols and marks representing ideas of number.
30–50 months	Uses some number names and number language spontaneously.
	Uses some number names accurately in play.
	Beginning to represent numbers using fingers, marks on paper or pictures.
	Shows curiosity about numbers by offering comments or asking questions.
	Shows an interest in numerals in the environment.
	Shows an interest in representing numbers.
40–60+ months	Recognise some numerals of personal significance.
	Recognises numerals 1 to 5.
	Counts actions or objects which cannot be moved.
	Counts objects to 10.
	Selects the correct numeral to represent 1 to 5.
	Counts an irregular arrangement of up to ten objects.
	Records, using marks that they can interpret and explain.

Active learning
Playing and talking about the game.

Problem solving skills
Making predictions about the result.
Recording the outcomes.
Turn-taking.

Encouraging discussion
Discussing who they think will win.
Discussing how to record the results.
Talking about the results at the end of a series of games.

Links to prior experiences
Talk about other dice games that they have played either in the setting or at home.

Possible misconceptions or difficulties
Mismatch between the dice roll and the number it represents. Use a large dice and count the dots by touching them.
Model the dice faces using counters and count the counters by touching them.

Subject knowledge for practitioners
Early counting skills.

Personal and emotional development
Cooperating and taking turns.
Being sensitive to others.
Work as part of a group.

Activity 5: Spiders

Setting up the activity: Read a story book about insects or watch a video together which explores insects. Ideally you could go for a mini-beast hunt outside and draw or take photographs of insects. Follow this up by drawing pictures or making models of the insects that children have seen.

Create an instruction sheet like the one to the right. Use two different sizes of pieces of clay for the body and head and sticks for the legs. These should be placed in a tray in the centre of a table.

Modelling material should be available on the table and books and images of insects.

Roll a spider

Dice	Symbol	Part
⚅	◯	body
⚃	○	head
⚄	𝄜	legs
⚂	𝄜	legs
⚁	𝄜	legs
⚀	𝄜	legs

What to do:
Play the 'make-a-spider' game with a group of children initially to model the process. Take it in turns to roll a dice. To start to build the spider you have to roll a 6 to build the body. Then a roll of 1, 2, 3 or 4 allows you to place a pair of legs on the body. A roll of 5 allows you to add the head. The game is won by the first person to complete a spider.

Recording:
Ask children to record the number of turns that they need to complete the insect in any way they want.

What to ask:
What number do you need to roll next?
How many more legs do you need?

Words to use:
What else comes in 'pairs?
How many legs?
How many more legs?

To develop the activity:
Create new games based on different insects.
Count in twos as the legs are placed on the body in pairs.

Mathematical development

Age range	What a child is learning
Birth–11 months	Notices changes in number of objects/images or sounds in group of up to 3.
8–20 months	Develops an awareness of number names through their enjoyment of action rhymes and songs that relate to their experience of numbers.
16–26 months	Says some counting words randomly.
22–36 months	Recites some number names in sequence.
	Creates and experiments with symbols and marks representing ideas of number.
30–50 months	Uses some number names and number language spontaneously.
	Uses some number names accurately in play.
	Beginning to represent numbers using fingers, marks on paper or pictures.
	Shows curiosity about numbers by offering comments or asking questions.
	Shows an interest in numerals in the environment.
	Shows an interest in representing numbers.
40–60+ months	Recognise some numerals of personal significance.
	Recognises numerals 1 to 5.
	Counts up to three or four objects by saying one number name for each item.
	Counts actions or objects which cannot be moved.
	Counts objects to 10.
	Counts out up to six objects from a larger group.
	Selects the correct numeral to represent 1 to 5, then 1 to 10 objects.
	Records, using marks that they can interpret and explain.

Active learning
Creating insects that they have seen on the mini-beast hunt or in books.
Playing a game.

Problem solving skills
Think of strategies to win the game.
Develop their own version of the game using a different insect.

Encouraging discussion
Talk about the mini-beasts they have seen on the walk or in books to decide which to make.
Compare the insects that they make.
Discuss who they think will win at different stages of the game.

Links to prior experiences
Representing and creating insects they have seen.
Talk about insects that children see at home or in the environment.
Talk about insects in favourite books or films.

Possible misconceptions or difficulties
Mismatch between the dice roll and the number it represents. Use a large dice and count the dots by touching them.
Model the dice faces using counters and count the counters by touching them.

Subject knowledge for practitioners
Names of common mini-beasts.
Early counting skills.

Personal and emotional development
Cooperating and taking turns; Speak about their insects.

Activity 6: Traffic jams

Setting up the activity: This can either take place indoors with toys vehicles or outside with the vehicles that children use (trikes, scooters and so on). If possible use a map of a street system.

Provide a large tray of toy vehicles including cars, trucks, vans, coaches and so on.

What to do:
Read a story such as *Red Car, Red Bus* by Susan Steggal which describes a journey in a car. Talk about journeys that the children make in cars. Allow the children to play freely with the vehicles. Talk about the directions that the vehicles are taking. Join in the free play. Start to create a traffic jam and talk about your own traffic jam. Describe the relative positions of vehicles and count how many of each vehicle there are in your traffic jam. Encourage children to create their own traffic jam.

Count the numbers of different types of vehicles. If appropriate encourage children to estimate how many of each vehicle there are.

Recording:
Children record the vehicles in their traffic jam in any way they wish.
Children classify the vehicles and record this.

What to ask:
Are there more cars than trucks?
How long is the jam?
What is at the front/back of the traffic jam?

Words to use:
Turn left/right.
Go straight on.
Next to . . .
In front of/behind.
First, second, third and so on.
Cardinal numbest for counting different vehicles.

To develop the activity:
Children can develop a story based on their play.
Record the different numbers of vehicles in each category.
Ask, "How many more cars than?"
Ask, "How many left if I take 2 away?"
Children develop their own calculation stories.

Mathematical development

Age range	What a child is learning
Birth–11 months	Notices changes in number of objects/images or sounds in group of up to 3.
8–20 months	Develops an awareness of number names through their experience of numbers.
16–26 months	Says some counting words randomly.
22–36 months	Recites some number names in sequence.
	Creates and experiments with symbols and marks representing ideas of number.
30–50 months	Uses some number names and number language spontaneously.
	Uses some number names accurately in play.
	Recites numbers in order to 10.
	Beginning to represent numbers using fingers, marks on paper or pictures.
	Shows curiosity about numbers by offering comments or asking questions.
	Shows an interest in numerals in the environment.
	Shows an interest in representing numbers.
40–60+ months	Recognise some numerals of personal significance.
	Recognises numerals 1 to 5.
	Counts up to three or four objects by saying one number name for each item.
	Counts actions or objects which cannot be moved.
	Counts objects to 10 and beginning to count beyond 10.
	Counts out up to six objects from a larger group.
	Selects the correct numeral to represent 10 objects.
	Counts an irregular arrangement of up to ten objects.
	Estimates how many objects they can see and checks by counting them.
	Records, using marks that they can interpret and explain.

Active learning
Playing with vehicles on a road map or driving vehicles around a road outside.

Problem solving skills
Telling a story linked to the activity. Representing a story with vehicles.
Classifying different sorts of vehicles and explaining the classification.

Encouraging discussion
Sharing stories and comparing classifications of vehicles.
Talk about experiences of journeys outside the setting.

Links to prior experiences
Talk about favourite films and books which include vehicles (fiction and non-fiction).
Talk about journeys on public transport (including bus numbers) or in cars.

Possible misconceptions or difficulties
Early counting misconceptions (see page 000 in Section 1).

Subject knowledge for practitioners
Model accurate mathematical vocabulary for shapes when drawing or creating the aliens.
Model counting accurately – touch the vehicles as you count them.
Model estimation skills – "I think there will be 6 cars" – then count them.

Personal and emotional development
Sharing vehicles during free play, being sensitive to others.
Speak about their ideas and share stories.
Work as part of a group.

Activity 7: Filling the grid

Setting up the activity: On a table place a grid with the numerals 1–10 on the grid

1	2	3	4	5	6	7	8	9	10

In a tray in the centre of the table place other items such as dice (6-sided and 10-sided if possible); sets of Numicon® pieces; connecting cubes; pictures with different numbers of objects on them from 1 to 10.

What to do:
Children work as a group to place all the objects in the appropriate place on the grid. Encourage turn taking and discussion of where to place the objects. Encourage children to go outside or walk around the classroom to find other objects that they can place in the grid.

Recording:
Encourage children to add their own drawings to the grid.

What to ask:
How many . . . are there?
Where will you put that? Why?
What is missing?
Is that in the correct place? How do you know?

Words to use:
The cardinal numbers 1 to 10.

To develop the activity:
Extend the grid beyond 10.

Mathematical development

Age range	What a child is learning
Birth–11 months	Notices changes in number of objects/images or sounds in group of up to 3.
8–20 months	Develops an awareness of number names through their experience of numbers.
16–26 months	Says some counting words randomly.
22–36 months	Recites some number names in sequence.
	Creates and experiments with symbols and marks representing ideas of number.
30–50 months	Uses some number names and number language spontaneously.
	Recites numbers in order to 10.
	Beginning to represent numbers using fingers, marks on paper or pictures.
	Shows curiosity about numbers by offering comments or asking questions.
	Shows an interest in representing numbers.
40–60+ months	Recognise some numerals of personal significance.
	Recognises numerals 1 to 5.
	Counts up to three or four objects by saying one number name for each item.
	Counts objects to 10, and beginning to count beyond 10.
	Selects the correct numeral to represent 1 to 10 objects.
	Counts an irregular arrangement of up to ten objects.
	Estimates how many objects they can see and checks by counting them.
	Records, using marks that they can interpret and explain.

Active learning
Encourage children to find objects which they can place in the grid.

Problem solving skills
Noticing which objects they still need to find.
Finding appropriate objects – estimating and then counting (for example, leaves on a branch) to place in correct place.
Thinking what type of object can be used.

Encouraging discussion
Talk about the decisions they are making and why they are placing objects in particular places.

Links to prior experiences
What do they know that comes in 2s, 3s, 4s and so on?
What numbers do they see in the environment?

Possible misconceptions or difficulties
Mismatch between written numbers and the numbers they represent. Count objects carefully by touching them.

Subject knowledge for practitioners
Model counting accurately – touch the objects as you count them.
Model estimation skills – "I think this will go with the 8 objects" then count to check.

Personal and emotional development
Planning activity together deciding what to collect.
Speak about their ideas when deciding what to collect.
Work as part of a group.

Activity 8: On your bike

Setting up the activity: Create a track in the outside area with numbered points of interest. This could be temporary using chalk and flags with the numbers on, or, ideally a permanent feature with numbers painted along the track at intervals. Place boxes or trays at each numbered point. Use a 'lollipop' style stop and go sign.

What to do:
The children should engage in free play on the trikes and scooters giving each other instructions about where to cycle to. Encourage them to give each other instructions. One of the children can use the lollipop sign to direct the other children. Encourage the children to use the numbers to direct people saying, "stop at number 2".

Recording:
Encourage children to create their own number signs to place around the track.

What to ask:
Who is first on the track?
Where are you going to stop?
Have you gone past 1/2/3?

Words to use:
Turn left/turn right/straight on.

To develop the activity:
Children can collect objects which they place in the appropriate trays. For example, they could place two pebbles in the tray at sign 2.

Mathematical development

Age range	What a child is learning
Birth–11 months	Notices changes in number of objects/images or sounds in group of up to 3.
8–20 months	Develops an awareness of number names through their enjoyment of action rhymes and songs that relate to their experience of numbers.
16–26 months	Says some counting words randomly.
22–36 months	Recites some number names in sequence. Creates and experiments with symbols and marks representing ideas of number.
30–50 months	Uses some number names and number language spontaneously. Uses some number names accurately in play. Beginning to represent numbers using fingers, marks on paper or pictures. Shows curiosity about numbers by offering comments or asking questions. Shows an interest in numerals in the environment. Shows an interest in representing numbers.
40–60+ months	Recognise some numerals of personal significance. Recognises numerals 1 to 5. Counts up to three or four objects by saying one number name for each item. Counts objects to 10. Selects the correct numeral to represent 1 to 5, then 1 to 10 objects. Counts an irregular arrangement of up to ten objects. Estimates how many objects they can see and checks by counting them. Records, using marks that they can interpret and explain.

Active learning
All the children take turns riding the trikes or scooters and directing the others using the stop/go sign.

Problem solving skills
Plan for alternative routes around the track.
Giving direction to go to particular stopping points.
Describing possible alternative routes to the same point.
Explaining which is the quickest route.

Encouraging discussion
Describe different routes to each other.
Making up stories that go with the routes they are taking

Links to prior experiences
Talking about their own journeys to and from school.
Talking about journeys in the car or on public transport and places/buildings that they pass.

Possible misconceptions or difficulties
Not recognising numerals represent numbers – model the correct vocabulary.

Subject knowledge for practitioners
How to develop early counting skills.

Personal and emotional development
Cooperating and taking turns on trikes and with stop/go sign.
Telling each other stories about journeys.
Work as part of a group.

Activity 9: Hopscotch

Setting up the activity: Create a hopscotch grid outside. Ideally this should be permanent. Alternatively
use chalk to create the grid. The children could
create the grid for you. You can also create a grid
inside using masking tape and number carpet tiles.
 You will need beanbags to throw onto the grid.

What to do:
There are several different games that can be
played. In all of the games children should count
as they hop.

1. Children take it in turns to throw the beanbag.
   They should throw the beanbag into square 1 first. Hop up and down the grid land-
   ing on one foot on 1, 4, 7 and 10 and 2 feet on 2, 3 and 5, 6 and 8, 9. When they
   return to square 1 they pick up the bean bag and hand it to the next person for their
   turn. This is repeated for each number.

2. Children take it in turns to throw the beanbag. They can throw it into any number.
   They hop up and down the grid collecting the beanbag on the way back down the
   grid. They score the number that the beanbag landed in. Each person has 5 goes and
   then adds up their total.

3. As above but the child should aim to make a total of exactly 20.

Recording:
The children should record the results of the game, either to make sure that everyone
keeps to turns or to keep score.

What to ask:
Whose turn is next? How do you know?
Which number do you want to land on next? Why?

Words to use:
Cardinal numbers 1 to 10. (One, two, three, four and so on.)

To develop the activity:
Use different totals for version 3 of the game.
Children can design their own games using the same grid.

Mathematical development

Age range	What a child is learning
Birth–11 months	Notices changes in number of objects/images or sounds in group of up to 3.
8–20 months	Develops an awareness of number names through their experience of numbers.
16–26 months	Says some counting words randomly.
22–36 months	Recites some number names in sequence.
	Creates and experiments with symbols and marks representing ideas of number.
30–50 months	Uses some number names and number language spontaneously.
	Uses some number names accurately in play.
	Recites numbers in order to 10.
	Beginning to represent numbers using fingers, marks on paper or pictures.
	Shows curiosity about numbers by offering comments or asking questions.
	Shows an interest in numerals in the environment.
	Shows an interest in representing numbers.
	Realises not only objects, but anything can be counted, including steps, claps or jumps.
40–60+ months	Recognise some numerals of personal significance.
	Recognises numerals 1 to 5.
	Counts actions or objects which cannot be moved.
	Counts objects to 10, and beginning to count beyond 10.
	Selects the correct numeral to represent 1 to 5, then 1 to 10 objects.
	Records, using marks that they can interpret and explain.

Active learning
Playing the game as a group.

Problem solving skills
Designing new games using the same grid and explaining the rules to others. Adapting the rules based on experience and feedback.

Encouraging discussion
Agreeing whose turn it is.
Agreeing on how to keep score.

Links to prior experiences
Talk about similar games that children might play at home.

Possible misconceptions or difficulties
Not recognising numerals represent numbers – model the correct vocabulary.

Subject knowledge for practitioners
How to develop early counting skills.

Personal and emotional development
Cooperating and taking turns on trikes and with stop/go sign.
Telling each other stories about journeys.
Work as part of a group.

Activity 10: Where do we live?

Setting up the activity: You will need large sheets of paper and art materials in the middle of the table to create a 2-dimensional map. Alternatively, use modelling materials to make houses which can be used to create a 3-dimensional map. This will need a large space or table-top in the setting.

What to do:
Go for a walk around the immediate school environment. Take photographs on the walk of key buildings. Make notes of the numbers on the house and the street names. Draw an example of a simple map of the local area.

The group can either create a 2-dimensional map of the walk that you went on. This should be the children's own version of a map. Avoid leading the children too much. They can use the photgraphs to add to the map.

If they are creating 3-dimensional models of the buildings, they can use the photographs as inspiration. The buildings that they make should then be placed on a 'map' which shows where they are in relation to each other.

Recording:
Ask children to record what they observe on the walk. They can use digital cameras to take photographs of key buildings.

What to ask:
Which buildings did we pass first?
What are the numbers on those buildings?
What did you notice about the numbers on the buildings?
What is the same and what is different about these two maps?

Words to use:
Shape vocabulary when describing the buildings.
Use the numbers that you see on the buildings even if these are over 20.

To develop the activity:
Increase the complexity and accuracy of the maps that you are creating.

Mathematical development

Age range	What a child is learning
Birth–11 months	Notices changes in number of objects/images or sounds in group of up to 3.
8–20 months	Develops an awareness of number names that relate to their experience of numbers.
16–26 months	Says some counting words randomly.
22–36 months	Recites some number names in sequence.
	Creates and experiments with symbols and marks representing ideas of number.
30–50 months	Uses some number names and number language spontaneously.
	Uses some number names accurately in play.
	Beginning to represent numbers using fingers, marks on paper or pictures.
	Shows curiosity about numbers by offering comments or asking questions.
	Shows an interest in numerals in the environment.
	Shows an interest in representing numbers.
	Realises not only objects, but anything can be counted, including steps, claps or jumps.
40–60+ months	Recognise some numerals of personal significance.
	Recognises numerals 1 to 5.
	Records, using marks that they can interpret and explain.

Active learning
Both the walk around the local environment and the drawing and modeling process ensure that children are engaged actively.

Problem solving skills
Deciding how to represent the map of the walk whether this be in 2-dimensions or 3-dimensions.
Evaluating the map as they create it.
Giving other groups feedback on their maps and comparing different maps.

Encouraging discussion
Circle time to discuss the walk and the things that they observed.
Evaluation of each other's maps.

Links to prior experiences
Relating the walk to the streets that they live on.
Talk about where else the children see maps.

Possible misconceptions or difficulties
There will be a developing understanding of how to draw maps. Accept all responses and focus on numeral recognition 1–10 and beyond as the key mathematical focus.

Subject knowledge for practitioners
Cardinal numbers 1–10 and positional language.

Personal and emotional development
Planning the mapping activity together and discussing what they noticed on the walk.
Listening carefully to others and taking their ideas on board.
Being confident to try new ideas based on feedback.
Working as part of a group.

Activity 11: What makes 5?

Setting up the activity: Create a table or a display board with a large numeral '5' at the centre. The group should have a box with a range of resources in it including toy vehicles, dinosaurs, teddy bears, Numicon®, Multilink®, Cuisenaire rods®, magnetic construction shapes, coins and so on.

What to do:
Use the questions below to prompt children to create '5' in as many different ways as they can.

- How many different ways can you make 5 using those bears?
- How many cars and how many trucks make 5? Are there any other ways you can make 5?
- Are there 5 different colours in the classroom?
- Can you see any '5's in the classroom
- What are your 5 favourite toys?
- Find something outside that shows '5'? (A leaf or a flower for example)
- Can you find a '5' in this magazine/newspaper?

Recording:
The children should record '5' in as many ways as they can and add these to the display table or to the display board.

What to ask:
Explain to me why that represents '5'.
Are there any other ways that you can make 5?

Words to use:
Use the terminology of grouping to make 5 as in 'one group of 3 and one group of 2'.

To develop the activity:
This activity can, and should, be repeated for all the numbers between 0–20 over the year in the setting.
Some children will be able to work with larger numbers.

Mathematical development

Age range	What a child is learning
Birth–11 months	Notices changes in number of objects/images or sounds.
8–20 months	Develops an awareness of number names through their enjoyment of action rhymes and songs that relate to their experience of numbers.
16–26 months	Says some counting words randomly.
22–36 months	Recites some number names in sequence.
	Creates and experiments with symbols and marks representing ideas of number.
30–50 months	Uses some number names and number language spontaneously.
	Uses some number names accurately in play.
	Beginning to represent numbers using fingers, marks on paper or pictures.
	Shows curiosity about numbers by offering comments or asking questions.
	Shows an interest in numerals in the environment.
	Shows an interest in representing numbers.
40–60+ months	Recognise some numerals of personal significance.
	Recognises numerals 1 to 5.
	Counts up to three or four objects by saying one number name for each item.
	Selects the correct numeral to represent 1 to 5, then 1 to 10 objects.
	Counts an irregular arrangement of up to ten objects.
	Estimates how many objects they can see and checks by counting them.
	Records, using marks that they can interpret and explain.

Active learning
Children take responsibility for the display and engage actively in creating the display

Problem solving skills
Deciding how to create the display.
Checking that the display is accurate.
Thinking about how to add to the display.
Comparing and discussing each other's contributions to the display.

Encouraging discussion
Talk about where children see the
numeral 5 in the environment.
Talk about different ways to make 5. The images show 1 + 4 and 2 + 3.

Links to prior experiences
Discuss where the children might see '5's at home. On a clock or on a calendar for example.

Possible misconceptions or difficulties
Miscounting up to 5. Model accurate counting for the children.

Subject knowledge for practitioners
Understanding of early counting development.

Personal and emotional development
Planning activity together and speaking about their ideas.
Confident to try new ideas suggested by peers.
Work as part of a group.

Activity 12: The shoe shop

Setting up the activity: Create a shoe shop in the role-play area. This should include shelves which are labelled with the sizes of shoes. A range of shoes that can be sorted and classified and a till with play money. If possible, go to a local shoe-shop and collect old empty shoe-boxes for sorting. There should also be a large white-board for the children to record their activity on. It may be appropriate to include dressing-up clothes for children to wear when they take on roles.

Include measuring equipment and paper for designing posters and for drawing around feet.

What to do:

Introduce the children to a range of activities they can explore in the role-play area. For example:

Finding their shoe-size by taking shoes off and reading label and comparing it to their friends. Ordering the drawings in order of size.

Sorting shoe boxes onto shelves and labelling the shelves with the size.

Counting the numbers of shoes in each size.

Classifying shoes by size, colour, use or any other criteria.

Making patterns using paint and the tread on the bottom of the shoes.

Role play shop assistant and someone buying shoes.

Recording:

The children should be encouraged to record the results from all of the above activities on a large white-board or flip-chart in the role play area.

What to ask:

What size are your shoes? How do you know?

What is the biggest/smallest shoe box size?

Where should that box go? How do you know?

How are you sorting those shoes? Which group does this pair of shoes belong too?

Words to use:

Shoe size – and then the appropriate number names.

Bigger/smaller/middle-sized.

To develop the activity:

Count in 2s using pairs of shoes as a stimulus. Classify doll's shoes, giant's shoes.

Mathematical development

Age range	What a child is learning
Birth–11 months	Notices changes in number of objects/images or sounds in group of up to 3.
8–20 months	Develops an awareness of number names that relate to their experience of numbers.
16–26 months	Says some counting words randomly.
22–36 months	Recites some number names in sequence.
	Creates and experiments with symbols and marks representing ideas of number.
30–50 months	Uses some number names and number language spontaneously.
	Uses some number names accurately in play.
	Recites numbers in order to 10.
	Beginning to represent numbers using fingers, marks on paper or pictures.
	Shows curiosity about numbers by offering comments or asking questions.
	Shows an interest in numerals in the environment.
	Shows an interest in representing numbers.
40–60+ months	Recognise some numerals of personal significance.
	Recognises numerals 1 to 5.
	Counts up to three or four objects by saying one number name for each item.
	Counts objects to 10, and beginning to count beyond 10.
	Counts out up to six objects from a larger group.
	Selects the correct numeral to represent 1 to 5, then 1 to 10 objects.
	Counts an irregular arrangement of up to ten objects.
	Estimates how many objects they can see and checks by counting them.
	Records, using marks that they can interpret and explain.

Active learning
The use of the role-play area for all of these activities supports active learning and engagement of all pupils.

Problem solving skills
Pupils take responsibility for their own learning and for recording the outcomes. They play different roles, sort shoes in different ways and discuss outcomes.

Encouraging discussion
Discussion should take place in and out of role. The shopkeeper and customer can discuss purchases; the shop owner can discuss the decisions they are taking to order and classify the shoes and the children out of role can discuss the records they are creating of the results of the activity.

Links to prior experiences
Talk about local shoe shops. If possible arrange a visit to a local shoe shop. This can be used as a stimulus for creating the role play area.

Possible misconceptions or difficulties
Not attaching correct number labels to numerals.
Not keeping shoes in pairs.

Subject knowledge for practitioners
Model the correct number language when working in the role-play area with the children.

Personal and emotional development
Cooperating and taking turns in different roles.
Planning the activity together and speaking and sharing ideas.
Being sensitive to others' needs in the role play area.

Activity 13: Ten green bottles

Setting up the activity: Use either plastic bottles which can be set up on a shelf, or pictures of bottles or ask children to draw their own green bottles which can be cut out and used for the song.

What to do:
Set up all the bottles in a row on a shelf or at the front of the classroom. Start singing together as a group:

> Ten green bottles standing on the wall
> Ten green bottles standing on the wall
> And if one green bottle should accidentally fall
> There'll be [remove one bottle – the class claps whilst you count the remaining bottles]
> One, two, three, four, five, six, seven, eight, nine green bottles standing on the wall.

Repeat with one bottle being removed each verse.

Recording:
Ask children to make a story book of the song. Write the lyrics so there is a new verse on each page. The children should provide the illustrations

What to ask:
How many bottles will be left at the end of the next verse?

Words to use:
Numbers 1–10.
Count on/count back.
One less than/one more than.

To develop the activity:
There are lots of different songs and rhymes which involve counting forwards and backwards. Research them and draw on parents' expertise and knowledge to learn rhymes that are relevant to the children's background. Include rhymes in different languages in multilingual classrooms.
Exploring bottles packed in crates – many bottles come in crates which are laid out as an array.

Mathematical development

Age range	What a child is learning
Birth–11 months	Notices changes in number of objects/images or sounds in group of up to 3.
8–20 months	Develops an awareness of number names through their enjoyment of action rhymes and songs that relate to their experience of numbers.
16–26 months	Says some counting words randomly.
22–36 months	Recites some number names in sequence.
	Creates and experiments with symbols and marks representing ideas of number.
30–50 months	Uses some number names and number language spontaneously.
	Uses some number names accurately in play.
	Recites numbers in order to 10.
	Beginning to represent numbers using fingers, marks on paper or pictures.
	Shows curiosity about numbers by offering comments or asking questions.
	Realises not only objects, but anything can be counted, including steps, claps or jumps.
40–60+ months	Recognise some numerals of personal significance.
	Recognises numerals 1 to 5.
	Counts up to three or four objects by saying one number name for each item.
	Counts actions or objects which cannot be moved.
	Counts objects to 10.
	Selects the correct numeral to represent 1 to 5, then 1 to 10 objects.
	Records, using marks that they can interpret and explain.

Active learning
Engaging in the song and joining in the actions ensures children are actively learning.

Problem solving skills
Agreeing how best to illustrate the song.
Work as a group to illustrate one of pages and agree how they wish to illustrate the verse.

Encouraging discussion
Talk about other counting songs that they know and sing at home.
Talk about ways to illustrate the song and agree on a way forward.

Links to prior experiences
What counting songs do they know, or have they heard?
Where did they hear them?

Possible misconceptions or difficulties
Errors in counting backwards – always counting forwards.
Repeating the song several times and using a number line to model counting backwards will be helpful.

Subject knowledge for practitioners
The development of early counting skills.

Personal and emotional development
Cooperating and joining in with the song.
Planning the illustration activity together and sharing ideas.
Listening to others' ideas.
Working as part of a group.

Activity 14: Egg box exploration

Setting up the activity: Collect egg boxes. If possible, collect boxes that hold 4 eggs, 6 eggs, 10 eggs and 12 eggs. Place them in the centre of the table with objects that can acts as 'eggs' – cubes, or beads, or other objects.

What to do:
Count the objects into the egg box one-by-one.
Take them out one at a time – sing a similar song to 10 green bottles as you remove the objects.
Check that the song is correct by counting the objects each time.
   Place the number labels 1–6; or 1–10 or 1–12 on the table in order. Children should place egg boxes with the correct number of objects in them next to the number

Recording:
The children should make their own drawings of the egg boxes and write the appropriate numeral next to it.

What to ask:
How many eggs are in that box?
How many empty holes are there?
How many will there be when I take another egg out?
How many will there be if I put another egg in?

Words to use:
How many?
How many more?
How many altogether?

To develop the activity:
Put 2 beads in each compartment to model multiplication facts for 2.
Put 3 beads in each compartment to model multiplication facts for 3.
And so on.

Mathematical development

Age range	What a child is learning
Birth–11 months	Notices changes in number of objects/images or sounds in group of up to 3.
8–20 months	Develops an awareness of number names through their enjoyment of action rhymes and songs that relate to their experience of numbers.
16–26 months	Says some counting words randomly.
22–36 months	Recites some number names in sequence. Creates and experiments with symbols and marks representing ideas of number.
30–50 months	Uses some number names and number language spontaneously. Uses some number names accurately in play. Recites numbers in order to 10. Beginning to represent numbers using fingers, marks on paper or pictures. Shows curiosity about numbers by offering comments or asking questions. Shows an interest in numerals in the environment. Shows an interest in representing numbers.
40–60+ months	Recognise some numerals of personal significance. Recognises numerals 1 to 5. Counts objects to 10, and beginning to count beyond 10. Selects the correct numeral to represent 1 to 5, then 1 to 10 objects. Records, using marks that they can interpret and explain.

Active learning
Ask the children to place eggs in the boxes and take them out to match the numerals so that they take responsibility for their learning. All children should join in the song.

Problem solving skills
Counting and checking there are the correct number of eggs in each box.
Writing their own number labels for the posters.

Encouraging discussion
Children should check each other's answers and give feedback on the drawings.

Links to prior experiences
Ask children if they have egg boxes at home.
What other similar receptacles are there? Baking trays for cup-cakes?

Possible misconceptions or difficulties
Errors in counting backwards – always counting forwards.
Repeating the song several times and using a number line to model counting backwards will be helpful.

Subject knowledge for practitioners
The development of early counting skills.

Personal and emotional development
Cooperating and joining in with the song.
Planning the illustration activity together and sharing ideas.
Listening to others' ideas.
Working as part of a group.

Activity 15: Guess how many

Setting up the activity: You need a cloth. About the size of a tea-towel and up to 20 small cubes or counters in a range of colours.

What to do:
Count the cubes or counters all together so that the children know how many there are in total. Explain that you are going to drop a handful on the table and then quickly cover them up. The children have to tell you how many they think you have dropped on the table.

Pick up a handful and drop them on the table. Before the children have time to count cover them with the cloth. Ask each child how many objects they think are under the cloth. When they have each guessed remove the cloth and count them. Ask the children to explain the strategies that they used.

Repeat several times with different numbers of objects and let the group carry on with the activity independently.

Recording:
Ask the children to record the game in any way they like. They should then talk about the image they have drawn with you and explain it to their peers.

What to ask:
Were you correct?
How close was your guess?
How did you work it out?

Words to use:
How many more?
How many less?
What is the biggest/smallest guess?

To develop the activity:
Once children have seen the number of cubes add/remove some whilst the cubes are covered by the cloth. The children have to tell you how many you have added/removed.

Mathematical development

Age range	What a child is learning
Birth–11 months	Notices changes in number of objects/images or sounds in group of up to 3.
8–20 months	Develops an awareness of number names through their enjoyment of action rhymes and songs that relate to their experience of numbers.
16–26 months	Says some counting words randomly.
22–36 months	Recites some number names in sequence. Creates and experiments with symbols and marks representing ideas of number.
30–50 months	Uses some number names and number language spontaneously. Uses some number names accurately in play. Recites numbers in order to 10. Beginning to represent numbers using fingers, marks on paper or pictures. Shows curiosity about numbers by offering comments or asking questions. Shows an interest in representing numbers.
40–60+ months	Recognise some numerals of personal significance. Recognises numerals 1 to 5. Counts up to three or four objects by saying one number name for each item. Counts objects to 10, and beginning to count beyond 10. Selects the correct numeral to represent 1 to 5, then 1 to 10 objects. Counts an irregular arrangement of up to ten objects. Estimates how many objects they can see and checks by counting them. Records, using marks that they can interpret and explain.

Active learning
Taking responsibility for continuing the activity once it has been modelled by the practitioner engages the learners actively in their learning.

Problem solving skills
Comparing answers and discussing and explaining the strategies they are using. Developing a new strategy based on listening to their peers.

Encouraging discussion
As above – discussing the strategies that they are using to estimate accurately.

Links to prior experiences
What numbers can they recognise without counting (numbers on dice or on dominoes for example).

Possible misconceptions or difficulties
Skills of estimation at early stages – allow these children to take the lead in counting the objects to check how accurate the estimates are.

Subject knowledge for practitioners
This activity develops 'subitising' skills. This is a term that was coined by Piaget and refers to the ability to be able to 'see' how many objects there are in a set without having to count them. There is research evidence to show that children who develop good subitising skills, or 'feel for number' are more likely to have long term success in mathematics than their peers whio do not develop these skills.

Personal and emotional development
Speak about their ideas and strategies.
Adapting their strategies based on discussion with peers.

6

Mainly number
Calculating

The activities in this section develop the following mathematical skills:

Age range	What a child is learning
Birth–11 months	Notices changes in number of objects/images or sounds in group of up to 3.
8–20 months	Has some understanding that things exist, even when out of sight.
16–26 months	Knows that things exist, even when out of sight. Says some counting words randomly.
22–36 months	Selects a small number of objects from a group when asked, for example, 'please give me one', 'please give me two'. Creates and experiments with symbols and marks representing ideas of number. Begins to make comparisons between quantities. Uses some language of quantities, such as 'more' and 'a lot'. Knows that a group of things changes quantity when something is added or taken away.
30–50 months	Beginning to represent numbers using fingers, marks on paper or pictures. Compares two groups of objects, saying when they have the same number. Shows an interest in number problems. Separates a group of three or four objects in different ways, beginning to recognise that the total is still the same.
40–60+ months	Counts out up to six objects from a larger group. Uses the language of 'more' and 'fewer' to compare two sets of objects. Finds the total number of items in two groups by counting all of them. Says the number that is one more than a given number. Finds one more or one less from a group of up to five objects, then ten objects. In practical activities and discussion, beginning to use the vocabulary involved in adding and subtracting. Records, using marks that they can interpret and explain. Begins to identify own mathematical problems based on own interests and fascinations.

Remember, children develop at their own rates, and in their own ways. These statements and their order should not be taken as necessary steps or checklists for individual children.

By the end of Year 1 children should:

> count reliably with numbers from 1 to 20, place them in order and say which number is one more or one less than a given number. Using quantities and objects, add and subtract two single-digit numbers and count on or back to find the answer. . . . solve problems, including doubling, halving and sharing.

Routine activities

Think through the routines of a school day and all the opportunities there are for sharing and for calculating, "how many more? or, "how many have I taken away? Also get used to using the language of comparison such as more than, less than and fewer. Most importantly allow children to explore these questions for themselves making marks to show what they have discovered.

Activity 16: Five little fish

Setting up the activity Provide finger puppets or other objects which can represent the fish swimming away. Alternatively, find a video of the song which you can use

What to do:
Teach the group the song modelling the use of the finger puppets or the other objects. Teach the children the actions that go with the song

> Five little fish went swimming one day
> Over the hill and far away
> Mummy/Daddy fish said, "It's time to come back"
> Only four fish came swimming back

Repeat with one fish fewer each verse.

Once the group have learned the song ask them to teach the rest of the class.

Recording:
Ask children to make a story book of the song. Write the lyrics so there is a new verse on each page. The children should provide the illustrations.

What to ask:
How many fish will be left at the end of the next verse?

Words to use:
Numbers 1–5.
Count on/count back.
One less than/one more than.

To develop the activity:
There are lots of different songs and rhymes which involve counting forwards and backwards. Research them and draw on parents' expertise and knowledge to learn rhymes that are relevant to the children's background. Include rhymes in different languages in multilingual classrooms.

Children can make-up their own number rhymes and songs which involve taking away one at a time.

Mathematical development

Age range	What a child is learning
Birth–11 months	Notices changes in number of objects/images or sounds in group of up to 3.
8–20 months	Has some understanding that things exist, even when out of sight.
16–26 months	Knows that things exist, even when out of sight. Says some counting words randomly.
22–36 months	Creates and experiments with symbols and marks representing ideas of number. Begins to make comparisons between quantities. Knows that a group of things changes quantity when something is added or taken away.
30–50 months	Beginning to represent numbers using fingers, marks on paper or pictures. Shows an interest in number problems.
40–60+ months	Uses the language of 'more' and 'fewer' to compare two sets of objects. Finds one more or one less from a group of up to five objects. In practical activities and discussion, beginning to use the vocabulary involved in adding and subtracting. Records, using marks that they can interpret and explain.

Active learning
Engaging in the song and joining in the actions ensures children are actively learning as does teaching the song to other children.

Problem solving skills
Agreeing how best to illustrate the song.
Agreeing the roles they will take when teaching the song.

Encouraging discussion
Talk about other counting songs that they know and sing at home.
Talk about ways to illustrate the song and agree on a way forward.

Links to prior experiences
What counting songs do they know, or have they heard?
Where did they hear them?

Possible misconceptions or difficulties
Errors in counting backwards – always counting forwards.
Repeating the song several times and using a number line to model counting backwards will be helpful.

Subject knowledge for practitioners
The development of early counting skills.

Personal and emotional development
Cooperating and joining in with the song.
Planning the illustration activity together and sharing ideas.
Listening to others' ideas.
Working as part of a group.

Activity 17: Fishing

Setting up the activity: Create a set of small laminated fish which can be placed in a shoe-box to act as a pond. If you can find a small toy net that would be great. This is even more fun played with objects in the water area outside and a real fishing net
Create the following set of cards.

Catch 1 fish (+)	Catch 2 fish (+)	Throw 1 fish back (–)	Throw 2 fish back (–)
Catch 1 fish (+)	Catch 3 fish (+)	Throw 1 fish back (–)	Throw 2 fish back (–)
Catch 2 fish (+)	Catch 3 fish (+)	Throw 1 fish back (–)	Throw 2 fish back (–)

The + cards and – cards should be on different coloured card and placed in two separate bags. One labelled (+) and the other labelled (-)

What to do:
To play the game the children take it in turns to pick cards. They first pick a (+) card and carry out that instruction. On the next turn they pick a (-) card. If they don't have enough fish to follow the instructions in that card they miss that turn.
At the end of 5 turns each they should see how many fish they have altogether.
Repeat the game and see if they can collect more fish as a group.

Recording:
The children should keep their own record of the score on a large white-board next to the 'fishing-pool'. They should be able to tell you what the score is after the game.

What to ask:
How many will you have left after you have followed that instruction?
What card do you want to pick next?
Who has the most/least fish?

Words to use:
More/less.
Most/fewest.
1 more/less; 2 more/less.
How many.

To develop the activity:
Ask the children how they would like to develop the activity. What new rules or cards could they introduce. The activity should be available for free play.

Mathematical development

Age range	What a child is learning
Birth–11 months	Notices changes in number of objects/images or sounds in group of up to 3.
8–20 months	Has some understanding that things exist, even when out of sight.
16–26 months	Knows that things exist, even when out of sight. Says some counting words randomly.
22–36 months	Selects a small number of objects from a group when asked, for example, 'please give me one', 'please give me two'. Creates and experiments with symbols and marks representing ideas of number. Begins to make comparisons between quantities. Uses some language of quantities, such as 'more' and 'a lot'. Knows that a group of things changes quantity when something is added or taken away.
30–50 months	Beginning to represent numbers using fingers, marks on paper or pictures. Compares two groups of objects, saying when they have the same number.
40–60+ months	Counts out up to six objects from a larger group. Uses the language of 'more' and 'fewer' to compare two sets of objects. Finds the total number of items in two groups by counting all of them. Says the number that is one more than a given number. Finds one more or one less from a group of up to five objects, then ten objects. In practical activities and discussion, beginning to use the vocabulary involved in adding and subtracting. Records, using marks that they can interpret and explain.

Active learning
Playing the game as a group involves the children in learning actively as they take turns and check each other's calculations.

Problem solving skills
Creating new rules and thinking through how to keep a record to make sure turn-taking takes places and the score is kept supports the development of problem solving skills

Encouraging discussion
Pupils should share the recording and discuss the best way to keep a record before starting the game. They will also talk about other experiences involving collecting things, fishing or fairground games.

Links to prior experiences
Talk about similar games. Perhaps visits to the fairground. Some children may go fishing at home or may have siblings of parents and carers who enjoy fishing. Those who enjoy fishing can come into the setting to talk about the hobby.

Possible misconceptions or difficulties
Making errors in calculation. A laminated number line next to the 'pond' will be helpful to model adding and subtracting as well as recounting the set of fish carefully.

Subject knowledge for practitioners
Support the children in calculating by using the fish. Physically remove or add the fish and then count by touching. Carefully model the use the vocabulary of 1 more than, 2 less than and so on.

Personal and emotional development
Cooperating and taking turns, planning and recording scores together by speaking about their ideas and listening to others carefully.

Activity 18: Cuisenaire® trucks

Setting up the activity: On a table collect together a series of vehicles including flat-bed trucks and other lorries or trucks that can be 'loaded'. There should also be a set of Cuisenaire® rods on the table. If you have a floor map of a road system the supports the children develop free play and narratives involving the trucks they have loaded.

Alternatively, this activity can take place outdoors with larger vehicles and a large set of Cuisenaire® rods

What to do:
Read a story or watch a video which involves a truck being loaded. This may be a tractor being loaded with bales of hay; trucks on a construction site delivering materials or collecting waste or any other delivery vehicles. Then model the story using the vehicles and load them using the Cuisenaire® rods

Recording:
Record the different loads by taking a photograph. Model the use of drawings to show the different loads possible in a truck. The children should keep their own records of the loads in any way they choose.

What to ask:
Which rods will fit?
What will you load on next?

Words to use:
Model relationships such as, "two reds make one purple".
Next to, on top of, beside, between.

To develop the activity:
Children can use the rods in free play to explore the relationships between the rods

Mathematical development

Age range	What a child is learning
Birth–11 months	Notices changes in number of objects/images or sounds in group of up to 3.
8–20 months	Has some understanding that things exist, even when out of sight.
16–26 months	Knows that things exist, even when out of sight.
	Says some counting words randomly.
22–36 months	Creates and experiments with symbols and marks representing ideas of number.
	Begins to make comparisons between quantities.
	Uses some language of quantities, such as 'more' and 'a lot'.
30–50 months	Beginning to represent numbers using fingers, marks on paper or pictures.
	Shows an interest in number problems.
40–60+ months	Uses the language of 'more' and 'fewer' to compare two sets of objects.
	In practical activities and discussion, beginning to use the vocabulary involved in adding and subtracting.
	Records, using marks that they can interpret and explain.
	Begins to identify own mathematical problems based on own interests and fascinations.

Active learning
Encourage children to see this as a play activity, telling stories about loading and unloading the trucks and using the rods to make the loads. Stacking them next to the trucks and noticing the relationships between the different coloured rods.

Problem solving skills
Trying out different arrangements of rods that will fit in or on a truck, considering alternatives and rejecting alternatives that will not work.

Encouraging discussion
Setting this activity within a story encourages discussion.

Links to prior experiences
Talk about the lorries that children see loading and unloading on the way to school. Lorries at shops, at the supermarket; at a building site; at a farm and so on.

Possible misconceptions or difficulties
Avoid labelling the rods with values. The white is not '1' and the red is not '2'. Use colours to talk about the relationships.

Subject knowledge for practitioners
It is important that practitioners understand how to use Cuisenaire® rods. See page 000 in the resources section.

Personal and emotional development
Planning activity together and speak about the stories that link with the loading and unloading
Working as part of a group and listening to others stories and ideas.

Activity 19: In the box

Setting up the activity: Place a small box or bag on a table. This should be opaque. Next to the box place up to 20 small objects. Cubes or counters or small toys.

What to do
Ask each child to pick up a handful of the objects. They should estimate how many they have picked up and then count them. Take one object from a child – place it in the box or bag saying, "I am taking one away. How many have you got now?" Count the objects. Ask, "How many in the box?" Take the object out of the box and recount to check that there are now the same number we started with. Repeat for each child.
    The children can than take on the role of the practitioner.

Recording:
At the end of the session ask the children to record the activity in any way they wish.

What to ask:
How many now?
How many all-together?

Words to use:
One more than.
One less than.
Add.
Take-away (also use subtract).

To develop the activity:
You can add and subtract two and three objects.

Mathematical development

Age range	What a child is learning
Birth–11 months	Notices changes in number of objects/images or sounds in group of up to 3.
8–20 months	Has some understanding that things exist, even when out of sight.
16–26 months	Knows that things exist, even when out of sight. Says some counting words randomly.
22–36 months	Selects a small number of objects from a group when asked, for example, 'please give me one', 'please give me two'. Creates and experiments with symbols and marks representing ideas of number. Begins to make comparisons between quantities. Knows that a group of things changes quantity when something is added or taken away.
30–50 months	Beginning to represent numbers using fingers, marks on paper or pictures. Compares two groups of objects, saying when they have the same number. Shows an interest in number problems.
40–60+ months	Counts out up to six objects from a larger group. Uses the language of 'more' and 'fewer' to compare two sets of objects. Says the number that is one more than a given number. Finds one more or one less from a group of up to five objects, then ten objects. In practical activities and discussion, beginning to use the vocabulary involved in adding and subtracting. Records, using marks that they can interpret and explain. Begins to identify own mathematical problems based on own interests and fascinations.

Active learning
Involving all the children in observing and discussing the activity engages them actively. It is important that they take on the practitioner's role to enhance this active learning.

Problem solving skills
As they continue with the activity children will begin to generalise the result of taking one way and then adding one back on. They will be able to predict the outcome without carrying out the activity.

Encouraging discussion
Encourage children to predict outcomes for each other and to record the outcomes and share the meanings of the marks they are making.

Links to prior experiences
Talk about occasions when children have to give objects away or are given things? When do they add and subtract as a part of everyday experience.

Possible misconceptions or difficulties
Children will not immediately realise that adding one back will mean we now have the same number. You may need to model this by placing one object close by rather than hiding it.

Subject knowledge for practitioners
Allow children to record this in any way they choose. They may draw pictures of the activity which are a literal representation, this is expected at this stage of development.

Personal and emotional development
Cooperating and taking turns, discussing ways of recording the activity together.

Activity 20: Number track games

Setting up the activity: Use a large number track up to 20 made of number carpet tiles. Ideally you should use a number track that is permanent and painted on the ground outside.

You also need a large foam dice that you have adapted so the faces show -1, +1, +2, +3, +2, -2.

What to do:
Play a game rolling the dice. The children follow the instructions on the dice. If a backwards move would take them past zero, then they miss that turn. They have to land exactly on the number at the end of the track to win.

Recording:
At the end of the activity ask children to record the activity in any way they wish.

What to ask:
What do you want to throw on the dice next?
Who do you think will win? Why?
Where will you end up when you jump on 2?

Words to use:
More than/less than.
Move forward/move backward.
Add/subtract.

To develop the activity:
This can take place as a free play activity. Use a range of different dice in different colours. The children can make up their own rules for the games and keep their own records.

Mathematical development

Age range	What a child is learning
Birth–11 months	Notices changes in number of objects/images or sounds in group of up to 3.
8–20 months	Has some understanding that things exist, even when out of sight.
16–26 months	Knows that things exist, even when out of sight. Says some counting words randomly.
22–36 months	Creates and experiments with symbols and marks representing ideas of number.
30–50 months	Beginning to represent numbers using fingers, marks on paper or pictures. Shows an interest in number problems.
40–60+ months	Says the number that is one more than a given number. In practical activities and discussion, beginning to use the vocabulary involved in adding and subtracting. Records, using marks that they can interpret and explain. Begins to identify own mathematical problems based on own interests and fascinations.

Active learning
Playing the game and devising new games as well as keeping records engages the children actively in their learning.

Problem solving skills
Developing rules for new games and devising ways of recording their results. Testing out new ideas for games and adapting their ideas.

Encouraging discussion
Encourage children to predict the results of the game and to talk about what they want the dice score to be on their next turn will support discussion.

Links to prior experiences
Talk about other games that the children play at home. Encourage them to bring them in and share them with their friends in the setting.

Possible misconceptions or difficulties
Miscounting on the number line by starting counting at the square they are already standing on.

Subject knowledge for practitioners
Model counting on and counting back by counting the steps that you take.

Personal and emotional development
Cooperating and taking turns.
Planning new rules for games together and listening to others' ideas.
Work as part of a group.

Activity 21: Bean bags in boxes

Setting up the activity: This activity can take place inside or outside. The larger the space the better. You will need some boxes of different sizes and bean-bags to throw into the boxes.

What to do:
The children should throw the bean bags into the boxes and see how many they can successfully throw into the box. They can throw into different size boxes and from different distances. Ask the children to record how many they throw into the box and how many miss. You can devise different scoring systems. They can subtract the number that miss from the number in the box to score or simply add the totals in the box. They can throw into two or three boxes and add the totals in each box and so on.

Recording:
Children should record the scores in any way they wish. They should explain the scores to you at the end of the game.

What to ask:
What are the rules of your game?
How do you score?
How many are in the box? How many are out of the box? How many altogether?

Words to use:
Altogether/total.
Add together.
Take away.

To develop the activity:
Encourage children to develop a range of scoring systems using the bean bags and the boxes.
    Ask them to find out what the furthest distance is at which they can be sure to throw the bean-bags into the boxes.

Mathematical development

Age range	What a child is learning
Birth–11 months	Notices changes in number of objects/images or sounds in group of up to 3.
8–20 months	Has some understanding that things exist, even when out of sight.
16–26 months	Knows that things exist, even when out of sight. Says some counting words randomly.
22–36 months	Selects a small number of objects from a group when asked, for example, 'please give me one', 'please give me two'. Creates and experiments with symbols and marks representing ideas of number. Begins to make comparisons between quantities. Uses some language of quantities, such as 'more' and 'a lot'. Knows that a group of things changes quantity when something is added or taken away.
30–50 months	Beginning to represent numbers using fingers, marks on paper or pictures. Compares two groups of objects, saying when they have the same number. Shows an interest in number problems.
40–60+ months	Uses the language of 'more' and 'fewer' to compare two sets of objects. Finds the total number of items in two groups by counting all of them. In practical activities and discussion, beginning to use the vocabulary involved in adding and subtracting. Records, using marks that they can interpret and explain. Begins to identify own mathematical problems based on own interests and fascinations.

Active learning
The children are actively engaged through playing the game and deciding on appropriate scoring and recording systems.

Problem solving skills
Devising appropriate scoring systems and agreeing rules for new games and new scoring systems. Exploring the relationship between distance away from the box and accuracy in throwing bean-bags.

Encouraging discussion
Children can discuss similar games they have played and make links with other areas such as sports activities.

Links to prior experiences
Children may have had similar experiences at fairs. You may be able to find video of similar games to show the children as inspiration for them to devise alternative games.

Possible misconceptions or difficulties
Some children may need support in throwing the bean-bags. They can stand as close as they like to the box so that they can be successful. Alternatively, children that find this very difficult can keep the record of the scores.

Subject knowledge for practitioners
Combining two groups as addition. Use the bean bags to model the process of combining two sets and then counting all.

Personal and emotional development
Cooperating and taking turns when playing the game and encouraging each other to be successful.
Planning the recording system together by listening to each other's ideas

Activity 22: Making groups

Setting up the activity: This is an activity that can be repeated as an everyday part of classroom routine. It is best carried out with groups of children, but the children can model the activity using cubes or any types of model people or toys.

What to do:
Roll a dice and ask children to get into groups of that number. If there are any 'left-over' count how many there are and then roll the dice and all the children join back in again. Encourage the children to play the game themselves using a large dice. This is best in a large space outside. They can also try to predict if they will be able to get into the groups 'without any left-over'.

Recording:
When children play the game independently ask them to record what they have found out. They can choose to record this in any way they choose and should explain their recording system to you at the end of the session.

What to ask:
How many groups?
How many in a group?
How many left over?

Words to use:
Numbers 1–6 when counting members of groups.
Numbers 1–10 when counting groups.
How many?
Left over.
Zero left over.

To develop the activity:
Ask children to predict if they will be able to make groups with zero left over.
Which numbers are possible for groups of 2, 3, 4, 5 and 6?

Mathematical development

Age range	What a child is learning
Birth–11 months	Notices changes in number of objects/images or sounds in group of up to 3.
8–20 months	Has some understanding that things exist, even when out of sight.
16–26 months	Knows that things exist, even when out of sight.
	Says some counting words randomly.
22–36 months	Creates and experiments with symbols and marks representing ideas of number.
	Uses some language of quantities, such as 'more' and 'a lot'.
	Knows that a group of things changes quantity when something is added or taken away.
30–50 months	Beginning to represent numbers using fingers, marks on paper or pictures.
	Compares two groups of objects, saying when they have the same number.
	Shows an interest in number problems.
	Separates a group of three or four objects in different ways, beginning to recognise that the total is still the same.
40–60+ months	Counts out up to six objects from a larger group.
	Uses the language of 'more' and 'fewer' to compare two sets of objects.
	In practical activities and discussion, beginning to use the vocabulary involved in adding and subtracting.
	Records, using marks that they can interpret and explain.
	Begins to identify own mathematical problems based on own interests and fascinations.

Active learning
This is a people mathematics activity and expects the children to move around the space. This engages them in the activity physically.

Problem solving skills
Testing out of it is possible to make groups with a given total without any left over.
Counting groups and rearranging the groups to make sure they have the correct number.
Devising ways of recording the outcomes.

Encouraging discussion
Ask children to talk about the activity whilst engaged in it, making predictions and testing out the outcomes. They should talk to each other to make sure they are forming the appropriate groups.

Links to prior experiences
Talk about times when people have to get into groups or teams. This may be team sports or may be other times during the school day when children are placed into groups.

Possible misconceptions or difficulties
Miscounting people as they are in a random order. Support individuals in counting by touching the head of each person as you count.

Subject knowledge for practitioners
Early counting skills – see page 000 in Section 1.

Personal and emotional development
Cooperating to complete the activity correctly.
Checking the numbers in the groups together.
Working as part of a small and a large group.

Activity 23: How many ears?

Setting up the activity: A box of toy animals or cartoon pictures of cats with ears and whiskers cut out and laminated.

Number labels 1 to 10 around the room or around a table of using cartoon images of cats.

What to do:
Ask children to place the correct number of cats next to a label. So, 1 cat next to the numeral 1, 2 next to the numeral 2 and so on.

Then ask them to place the cats so there are the correct number of ears. Children should explain why some numbers are possible and some are impossible.

Recording:
Children should record what they have found out in any way they choose. Ask the group to share their jottings with the rest of the class at the end of their exploration and explain what they have found out.

What to ask:
How many cats?
How many ears?
Tell me about what you have found out?

Words to use:
Count in ones.
Count in twos.

To develop the activity:
You can set any criteria for sorting – number of ears, number of whiskers, number of legs and ask children to explore the number patterns.

Mathematical development

Age range	What a child is learning
Birth–11 months	Notices changes in number of objects/images or sounds in group of up to 3.
8–20 months	Has some understanding that things exist, even when out of sight.
16–26 months	Knows that things exist, even when out of sight. Says some counting words randomly.
22–36 months	Creates and experiments with symbols and marks representing ideas of number. Begins to make comparisons between quantities. Uses some language of quantities, such as 'more' and 'a lot'.
30–50 months	Beginning to represent numbers using fingers, marks on paper or pictures. Compares two groups of objects, saying when they have the same number. Shows an interest in number problems.
40–60+ months	Counts out up to six objects from a larger group. Uses the language of 'more' and 'fewer' to compare two sets of objects. Finds the total number of items in two groups by counting all of them. In practical activities and discussion, beginning to use the vocabulary involved in adding and subtracting. Records, using marks that they can interpret and explain. Begins to identify own mathematical problems based on own interests and fascinations.

Active learning
Children moving round the room placing toys next to number labels.

Problem solving skills
Devising ways to record the learning.
Exploring which numbers and which are not possible

Encouraging discussion
Children should work together and discuss the patterns that they are noticing – or explain why it is not possible to have '3 ears'.

Links to prior experiences
Share stories of pets and other animals.
Talk about visits to a zoo.
What animals do children have experience of?
Children can make up mathematics stories about their pets or other animals

Possible misconceptions or difficulties
Counting pairs of ears as '1' as the ears are on one cat. Model counting the ears separately by touching them.

Subject knowledge for practitioners
You can introduce the terminology of odd and even numbers at this stage but do not expect children to have a clear understanding at this stage.

Personal and emotional development
Planning and discussing the outcomes of the activity together.
Confident to try new ideas to test out possibilities.
Work as part of a group.

Activity 24: Socks on a line

Setting up the activity: Set up a washing line across the front of the classroom or in the role-play area. Pairs of socks should be rolled together and placed in a washing basket. This is an ideal activity to take place outside where a real washing line and washing basket can be set up.

What to do:
Roll a dice and ask a child to count out this number of pairs of socks. Then ask them to unroll the socks and peg them out on the line, counting as they peg them out. The whole class should count together.

Repeat the activity several times. Children can discuss in pairs how many socks they think there might be. They can use number lines to help them think this through.

Introduce the idea of 'odd socks' by telling a story about losing a sock. Peg out 3 pairs and one odd sock and so on.

Recording:
Encourage children to continue to carry out the activity in the role play area or outside. Provide a white board or flip chart to record. The role play area can be set up as a launderette.

What to ask:
How many pairs?
How many socks?
Are there any odd socks?

Words to use:
Pair.
Total.
Even.
Odd.

To develop the activity:
Explore number of arms and number of shirts and other number patterns when hanging washing on a line.

Mathematical development

Age range	What a child is learning
Birth–11 months	Notices changes in number of objects/images or sounds in group of up to 3.
8–20 months	Has some understanding that things exist, even when out of sight.
16–26 months	Knows that things exist, even when out of sight. Says some counting words randomly.
22–36 months	Selects a small number of objects from a group when asked, for example, 'please give me one', 'please give me two'. Creates and experiments with symbols and marks representing ideas of number. Begins to make comparisons between quantities. Knows that a group of things changes quantity when something is added or taken away.
30–50 months	Beginning to represent numbers using fingers, marks on paper or pictures. Shows an interest in number problems.
40–60+ months	Counts out up to six objects from a larger group. Uses the language of 'more' and 'fewer' to compare two sets of objects. Says the number that is one more than a given number. Finds one more or one less from a group of up to five objects, then ten objects. In practical activities and discussion, beginning to use the vocabulary involved in adding and subtracting. Records, using marks that they can interpret and explain. Begins to identify own mathematical problems based on own interests and fascinations.

Active learning
Carrying out the activity by pegging out the socks as the whole class ensures that children will be engaged actively in the process. Make sure all children have a turn at pegging out at some stage.

Problem solving skills
Exploring the number patterns when pegging out pairs of socks and relationship between how many pairs and how many socks.
Exploring the difference that having an odd sock makes.

Encouraging discussion
Children can discuss in pairs or in small groups how to record what they are finding out and predict how many socks there will be for a given number of pairs.

Links to prior experiences
Talk about other things that come in pairs.
Talk about getting dressed and where socks are kept.
Visits to the launderette – or helping with the washing at home.

Possible misconceptions or difficulties
Confusion between counting '2 things', i.e. a pair, as a single thing.

Subject knowledge for practitioners
For most children this is a great practical way for extending counting skills. Some will make the connections between pairs and multiples of 2 but don't expect this – or overtly teach it.

Personal and emotional development
Cooperating and taking turns in pegging out socks.
Speak about their predictions for how many socks.
Work as part of a small and a large group.

Activity 25: Cuisenaire® trains

Setting up the activity: You need a set of Cuisenaire® rods in the centre of the table. You can use a large set of rods if they are available.

What to do:
Allow the children free play with the rods. They should use them to create patterns or build towers or buildings. After some time in free play model a Cuisenaire® train. This is when you lay the rods end to end.

Encourage children to make as many different trains as they can. Ask how many different trains they can make using just the red and white rods?

Recording:
Use photographs to record the trains that the children make. Encourage children to record the results for themselves.

What to ask:
Are there any other trains that are the same length?
Have you found them all?
How do you know?

Words to use:
Equivalent.
Same length.
Train.

To develop the activity:
Explore all the different trains which are equivalent to a single rod of any colour.

Mathematical development

Age range	What a child is learning
Birth–11 months	Notices changes in number of objects/images or sounds in group of up to 3.
8–20 months	Has some understanding that things exist, even when out of sight.
16–26 months	Knows that things exist, even when out of sight.
22–36 months	Creates and experiments with symbols and marks representing ideas of number. Begins to make comparisons between quantities. Uses some language of quantities, such as 'more' and 'a lot'. Knows that a group of things changes quantity when something is added or taken away.
30–50 months	Beginning to represent numbers using fingers, marks on paper or pictures. Compares two groups of objects, saying when they have the same number. Shows an interest in number problems. Separates a group of three or four objects in different ways, beginning to recognise that the total is still the same.
40–60+ months	Uses the language of 'more' and 'fewer' to compare two sets of objects. In practical activities and discussion, beginning to use the vocabulary involved in adding and subtracting. Records, using marks that they can interpret and explain. Begins to identify own mathematical problems based on own interests and fascinations.

Active learning
The movement of the rods and the matching of lengths engages children actively in their learning. Free play is important as a way of exploring the properties of the rods.

Problem solving skills
Exploring all the different trains of equivalent lengths.
Matching trains to single rods and then finding alternative trains.

Encouraging discussion
Learners discuss which trains are equivalent, which single rods they are equivalent to and which are longest and which are shortest.

Links to prior experiences
Make links to measurement activities.

Possible misconceptions or difficulties
Children may not match the ends of the rods to compare lengths.

Subject knowledge for practitioners
Ways to develop mathematics understanding using Cuisenaire® rods. See resources section, page 000.

Personal and emotional development
Planning activity together and comparing results.
Speak about their ideas and solutions to finding equivalent trains.

7

Mainly shape and space

The activities in this section develop the following mathematical skills

Age range	What a child is learning
Birth–11 months	Babies' early awareness of shape and space grows from their sensory awareness and opportunities to observe objects and their movements, and to play and explore.
8–20 months	Recognises shapes in meaningful contexts.
16–26 months	Attempts, sometimes successfully, to fit shapes into spaces on inset boards or jigsaw puzzles.
	Uses blocks to create their own simple structures and arrangements.
22–36 months	Notices simple shapes and patterns in pictures.
	Beginning to categorise objects according to properties such as shape.
	Begins to use the language of shape.
30–50 months	Shows an interest in shape and space by playing with shapes or making arrangements with objects.
	Shows awareness of similarities of shapes in the environment.
	Shows interest in shape by sustained construction activity or by talking about shapes or arrangements.
	Shows interest in shapes in the environment.
	Uses shapes appropriately for tasks.
	Beginning to talk about the shapes of everyday objects, e.g. 'round' and 'tall'.
40–60+ months	Beginning to use mathematical names for 'solid' 3D shapes and 'flat' 2D shapes, and mathematical terms to describe shapes.
	Selects a particular named shape.
	Uses familiar objects and common shapes to create and recreate patterns and build models.

Remember, children develop at their own rates, and in their own ways. These statements and their order should not be taken as necessary steps or checklists for individual children.

By the end of Year 1 children should have been taught to:

recognise and name common 2-D and 3-D shapes, including 2-D shapes [for example, rectangles (including squares), circles and triangles] and 3-D shapes [for example, cuboids (including cubes), pyramids and spheres] and to describe position, direction and movement, including whole, half, quarter and three-quarter turns.

Routine activities

Whenever children are engaged in free play with construction materials there are opportunities to talk about the shapes using the mathematical names. Use the names in play, for example, "Can you pass me that blue cube." "I need a pyramid – can you see one?"

Similarly talk about shapes in patterns around the classroom or on walks that you go on with the children. It will become second nature to notice shapes wherever you are. You can also take photographs of shapes that you find in the environment when you are away from school to share with children. They can create 'Holiday shape' books themselves with their parents.

Activity 26: Stars

Setting up the activity: Find patterns which include stars in the pattern, either wallpaper or fabric. If possible have several different patterns, some on fabric and some on paper.

You will also need art materials and paper for drawing stars. You can cut out stars or ask children to cut out stars to create displays.

What to do:
Initially, ask the children to sort the different patterns using any criteria that they choose. Once they have sorted the patterns ask them to tell you what criteria they have used. Then ask them to repeat the activity using a different set of criteria.

Recording:
Children should record the classification activity in any way they choose – they may choose to take photographs. This allows them to talk about the criteria they have used later. You can also use these images for display.

Use the stars that are drawn to create a display and to create a word-wall using key words.

What to ask:
What is the same and what is different about these stars?
Can you draw another star that would fit in this group?

Words to use:
Classify.
Points/vertex/vertices.
Edges.
Straight line.
Centre.

To develop the activity:
Observe different stars and talk about their properties.

Mathematical development

Age range	What a child is learning
Birth–11 months	Babies' early awareness of shape and space grows from their sensory awareness and opportunities to observe objects and their movements, and to play and explore.
8–20 months	Recognises shapes in meaningful contexts.
16–26 months	Attempts, sometimes successfully, to fit shapes into spaces on inset boards or jigsaw puzzles. Uses blocks to create their own simple structures and arrangements.
22–36 months	Notices simple shapes and patterns in pictures. Beginning to categorise objects according to properties such as shape. Begins to use the language of shape.
30–50 months	Shows an interest in shape and space by playing with shapes or making arrangements with objects. Shows awareness of similarities of shapes in the environment. Shows interest in shape by sustained construction activity or by talking about shapes or arrangements. Shows interest in shapes in the environment. Uses shapes appropriately for tasks. Beginning to talk about the shapes of everyday objects, e.g. 'round' and 'tall'.
40–60+ months	Beginning to use mathematical names for 'solid' 3D shapes and 'flat' 2D shapes, and mathematical terms to describe shapes. Uses familiar objects and common shapes to create and recreate patterns and build models.

Active learning
Both the physical action of moving material and images around to classify them and the creation of their own stars engage the children actively in the learning.

Problem solving skills
Exploring similarities and differences and describing properties involve making generalisations and close observations. These are problem solving skills.

Encouraging discussion
Children should describe the criteria they are using to sort stars with each other agreeing the classifications. They can also talk about the properties of the stars they are drawing.

Links to prior experiences
Talk about favourite films and books that contain stars.
Compare stars to other shapes that they see around them.
Look out for stars in the environment either in the setting or at home.

Possible misconceptions or difficulties
Careful use of language to help with pronunciation of words.

Subject knowledge for practitioners
Become confident in your own use of the vocabulary of shape. See page 000.

Personal and emotional development
Planning classification activity together and agreeing criteria.
Confident to try new ideas when reclassifying the stars.
Work as part of a group.

Activity 27: Hide and seek

Setting up the activity: You need a box of 3-dimensional shapes or a selection of building blocks and a small bag or a box which will hold one shape so that it cannot be seen

What to do:
Show the children the 3-dimensional shapes. Give them out one between a pair of children. They should look at and feel the shape and talk about the properties. Collect the shapes back in and select one without showing the children. Put it in the bag or box. One of the children should leave the room or close their eyes. Another child then hides the shape somewhere in the classroom. When the child comes back into the classroom or opens their eyes the rest of the class have to guide them to the hidden shape by giving directions.

   Once the shape has been found the child should feel the shape without looking at it and describe it. The other children should guess which shape it is. Have copies of the shapes so that the children can point to the shape that they think it is if they can't remember the name.

   The child who correctly guesses the shape takes the next turn in finding the hidden shape.

Recording:
One group should record who has had a turn to make sure that it is fair. They can also record "how long' it takes to find the shape each time. This might link to how many different instructions are given.

What to ask:
Is it flat?
Is it curved?
How many edges/faces/vertices?

Words to use:
Use the mathematical names for the shapes.
Flat face, curved face.
Edges, faces, vertices/corners.
Straight edge.

To develop the activity:
Use a wider range of shapes including 2-dimensional shapes. Use increasingly technical language.

Mathematical development

Age range	What a child is learning
Birth–11 months	Babies' early awareness of shape and space grows from their sensory awareness and opportunities to observe objects and their movements, and to play and explore.
8–20 months	Recognises shapes in meaningful contexts.
16–26 months	Attempts, sometimes successfully, to fit shapes into spaces on inset boards or jigsaw puzzles. Uses blocks to create their own simple structures and arrangements.
22–36 months	Beginning to categorise objects according to properties such as shape. Begins to use the language of shape.
30–50 months	Shows interest in shape by sustained construction activity or by talking about shapes or arrangements. Uses shapes appropriately for tasks. Beginning to talk about the shapes of everyday objects, e.g. 'round' and 'tall'.
40–60+ months	Beginning to use mathematical names for 'solid' 3D shapes and 'flat' 2D shapes, and mathematical terms to describe shapes. Selects a particular named shape.

Active learning
Giving instructions and being the 'hider' or the 'finder' makes sure that all the children are actively engaged in the activity and in learning.

Problem solving skills
Giving precise instructions to allow children to find the hidden object.
Describing properties carefully or using the properties to decide which shape is being described.

Encouraging discussion
Ask children to talk about the shapes that they are exploring at the beginning of the activity.
Children can discuss the possibilities after each property is described. Which shapes could it be? Which shapes do not fit this property?

Links to prior experiences
What 3-dimensional shapes can children see around the setting?
What 3-dimensional shapes can children on their walk or journey home form the setting?

Possible misconceptions or difficulties
Careful use of language to help with pronunciation of words.

Subject knowledge for practitioners
Become confident in your own use of the vocabulary of shape. See page 000.

Personal and emotional development
Working together to give accurate instructions.
Work as part of a pair to discuss the properties.

Activity 28: The feely bag

Setting up the activity: You need a box of 2-dimensional shapes and a small bag or a box which will hold one shape so that it cannot be seen.

What to do:
Show the children the shapes. Find out if they know the names of any of the shapes. Give them out one between a pair of children. They should look at and feel the shape and talk about the properties. Collect the shapes back in and put one of them in the bag or box without showing the class. One of the children should come to the front and feel the shape in the bag without looking at it and describe its properties. The other children should guess which shape it is. Have copies of the shapes so that the children can point to the shape that they think it is if they can't remember the name. The child who correctly guesses the shape takes the next turn in describing the shape in the feely bag.

Recording:
One group should record who has had a turn to make sure that it is fair. They can also record 'how long' it takes to find the shape each time. This might link to how many different instructions are given.

What to ask:
Has it got straight/curved edges?
How many edges/vertices?

Words to use:
Use the mathematical names for the shapes.
Straight/curved edge.
Edges, vertices/corners.

To develop the activity:
Use a wider range of shapes and use increasingly technical language.

Mathematical development

Age range	What a child is learning
Birth–11 months	Babies' early awareness of shape and space grows from their sensory awareness and opportunities to observe objects and their movements, and to play and explore.
8–20 months	Recognises shapes in meaningful contexts.
16–26 months	Attempts, sometimes successfully, to fit shapes into spaces on inset boards or jigsaw puzzles.
	Uses blocks to create their own simple structures and arrangements.
22–36 months	Beginning to categorise objects according to properties such as shape.
	Begins to use the language of shape.
30–50 months	Shows interest in shape by sustained construction activity or by talking about shapes or arrangements.
	Uses shapes appropriately for tasks.
	Beginning to talk about the shapes of everyday objects, e.g. 'round' and 'tall'.
40–60+ months	Beginning to use mathematical names for 'solid' 3D shapes and 'flat' 2D shapes, and mathematical terms to describe shapes.
	Selects a particular named shape.

Active learning
Describing and interpreting the properties makes sure that all the children are actively engaged in the activity and in learning.

Problem solving skills
Describing properties carefully or using the properties to decide which shape is being described.

Encouraging discussion
Ask children to talk about the shapes that they are exploring at the beginning of the activity.

Children can discuss the possibilities after each property is described. Which shapes could it be? Which shapes do not fit this property?

Links to prior experiences
What 2-dimensional shapes can children see around the setting?
What 2-dimensional shapes can children on their walk or journey home form the setting?

Possible misconceptions or difficulties
Careful use of language to help with pronunciation of words.

Subject knowledge for practitioners
Become confident in your own use of the vocabulary of shape. See page 000.

Personal and emotional development
Working together to give accurate instructions.
Work as part of a pair to discuss the properties.

Activity 29: A shape-walk

Setting up the activity: This activity involves a walk in the environment close to the school. It does not need any planning apart from making sure there are sufficient adults to accompany the children and that they have all been briefed that the aim is not to simply tell the children the names of the shapes they see.

The children will need a way of recording the shapes that they see. This could be digital cameras or simply a clip-board and paper.

What to do:
Walk around the streets close to the school. Adults should support children in recording the different shapes that they see. Avoid naming the shapes unless the children use the names first. The process will be that the children will research the names when returning to school. Make sure that complex and compound shapes are recorded including at least one whose name the adults don't know.

On returning to school the children use posters and books to find the shapes that they saw. The adults can read the names of the shapes for the children if needed. The children should then draw the shapes and cut them out.

Create posters of the shapes and annotate the posters with the names. Discuss the properties of the shapes and add these properties to the posters.

Recording:
Children make copies of the shapes that they have recorded whilst on the walk.

What to ask:
Has it got straight/curved edges?
How many edges/vertices?

Words to use:
Use the mathematical names for the shapes.
Straight/curved edge.
Edges, vertices/corners.
Flat face, curved face.
Edges, faces, vertices/corners.
Straight edge.

To develop the activity:
Create shape books with the children.

Mathematical development

Age range	What a child is learning
Birth–11 months	Babies' early awareness of shape and space grows from their sensory awareness and opportunities to observe objects and their movements, and to play and explore.
8–20 months	Recognises shapes in meaningful contexts.
16–26 months	Attempts, sometimes successfully, to fit shapes into spaces on inset boards or jigsaw puzzles.
	Uses blocks to create their own simple structures and arrangements.
22–36 months	Beginning to categorise objects according to properties such as shape.
	Begins to use the language of shape.
30–50 months	Shows interest in shape by sustained construction activity or by talking about shapes or arrangements.
	Uses shapes appropriately for tasks.
	Beginning to talk about the shapes of everyday objects, e.g. 'round' and 'tall'.
40–60+ months	Beginning to use mathematical names for 'solid' 3D shapes and 'flat' 2D shapes, and mathematical terms to describe shapes.
	Selects a particular named shape.

Active learning
Walking and observing shapes as well as describing and interpreting the properties makes sure that all the children are actively engaged.

Problem solving skills
Describing the properties of the shapes they have observed carefully and talking about similarities and differences.
Choosing which shapes to record and how to record them.

Encouraging discussion
Ask children to talk about the shapes that they are recording.
Children can discuss the possible names for the shapes when they research them back in the setting.

Links to prior experiences
What 2- and 3-dimensional shapes can children see around the setting?
What 2- and 3-dimensional shapes can children on their walk or journey home form the setting?

Possible misconceptions or difficulties
Careful use of language to help with pronunciation of words.

Subject knowledge for practitioners
Become confident in your own use of the vocabulary of shape. See page 000.

Personal and emotional development
Working together to select which shapes to record.
Work as part of a pair to discuss the properties.

Activity 30: Wrapping paper

Setting up the activity: Collect several different types of wrapping paper and cut into different sized rectangles including squares and oblongs (an oblong is a rectangle that is not a square – a square is a type of rectangle). Try to include some wrapping paper that has geometric shapes as part of the design. Put the pieces of wrapping paper in a pile in the centre of the table.

What to do:
Ask the children to sort the pieces of wrapping paper using any criteria that they choose. Once they have done this once ask them to tell you what criteria they have used. Then ask them to repeat the activity using a different set of criteria.

Recording:
Children should record the classification activity in any way they choose – they may choose to take photographs. This allows them to talk about the criteria they have used later. You can also use these images for display.

They should then design some wrapping paper of their own using the art materials. Invite the children to create wrapping paper for a mathematics present and so include some geometrical shapes.

What to ask:
What is the same and what is different about these pieces of wrapping paper?
What is the same and what is different about these shapes?

Words to use:
Classify.
Points/vertex/vertices.
Edges.
Straight line/curved line.
Centre.

To develop the activity:
Look at patterns around the school or take photographs of patterns near to the school and make displays to talk about the properties of the shapes.

Mathematical development

Age range	What a child is learning
Birth–11 months	Babies' early awareness of shape and space grows from their sensory awareness and opportunities to observe objects and their movements, and to play and explore.
8–20 months	Recognises shapes in meaningful contexts.
16–26 months	Attempts, sometimes successfully, to fit shapes into spaces on inset boards or jigsaw puzzles. Uses blocks to create their own simple structures and arrangements.
22–36 months	Notices simple shapes and patterns in pictures. Beginning to categorise objects according to properties such as shape. Begins to use the language of shape.
30–50 months	Shows an interest in shape and space by playing with shapes or making arrangements with objects. Shows awareness of similarities of shapes in the environment. Shows interest in shape by sustained construction activity or by talking about shapes or arrangements. Shows interest in shapes in the environment. Uses shapes appropriately for tasks. Beginning to talk about the shapes of everyday objects, e.g. 'round' and 'tall'.
40–60+ months	Beginning to use mathematical names for 'solid' 3D shapes and 'flat' 2D shapes, and mathematical terms to describe shapes. Uses familiar objects and common shapes to create and recreate patterns and build models.

Active learning
The physical action of moving the paper around to classify the pieces of paper and the creation of their own wrapping paper engage the children actively in the learning.

Problem solving skills
Exploring similarities and differences and describing properties of the shapes that they see involve making generalisations and making close observations. These are problem solving skills.

Encouraging discussion
Children should describe the criteria they are using to sort the wrapping paper with each other and agree the classifications. They can also talk about the properties of the shapes in the wrapping paper they are designing.

Links to prior experiences
Look for patterns on the journey to and from school – take photographs to talk about the properties.
Look for patterns around school.
Look for patterns at home – take photographs to talk about the properties.

Possible misconceptions or difficulties
Careful use of language to help with pronunciation of words.

Subject knowledge for practitioners
Become confident in your own use of the vocabulary of shape. See page 000.

Personal and emotional development
Planning classification activity together and agreeing criteria.
Confident to try new ideas when reclassifying the pieces of paper.
Work as part of a group.

Activity 31: Rope shapes

Setting up the activity: You need a large outdoor space and children – that's all! The children also need a way of recording the shapes that they are making.

What to do:
Before you go outside or into the large space that you are going to use agree which children will take responsibility for recording the shapes. They can use clip-boards and sheets of paper.

Once you are in the space lay out the rope in a line. Explain that the children are going to make shapes out of the ripe by holding it and moving to make the shape themselves. Ask the children to make the following shapes:

- Circle
- Square
- Rectangle
- A different rectangle ('longer and thinner' for example)
- A triangle
- A different triangle
- A triangle whose sides are the same length
- A triangle whose sides are different lengths

Recording:
Share the records from the activity outside and ask each group to draw three of the shapes that they made outside. The activity ends with each group describing the shapes they have drawn.

What to ask:
What is the same and what is different about the shapes that you have drawn.
Can you draw another shape that shares a property with that shape?

What to ask:
Has it got straight/curved edges?
How many edges/vertices?

Words to use:
Use the mathematical names for the shapes.
Straight/curved edge.
Edges, vertices/corners.

To develop the activity:
Create shape books with the children.

Mathematical development

Age range	What a child is learning
Birth–11 months	Babies' early awareness of shape and space grows from their sensory awareness and opportunities to observe objects and their movements, and to play and explore.
8–20 months	Recognises shapes in meaningful contexts.
16–26 months	Attempts, sometimes successfully, to fit shapes into spaces on inset boards or jigsaw puzzles.
	Uses blocks to create their own simple structures and arrangements.
22–36 months	Beginning to categorise objects according to properties such as shape.
	Begins to use the language of shape.
30–50 months	Shows interest in shape by sustained construction activity or by talking about shapes or arrangements.
	Uses shapes appropriately for tasks.
	Beginning to talk about the shapes of everyday objects, e.g. 'round' and 'tall'.
40–60+ months	Beginning to use mathematical names for 'solid' 3D shapes and 'flat' 2D shapes, and mathematical terms to describe shapes.
	Selects a particular named shape.

Active learning
Making the shapes physically engages the children actively in thinking about the properties of shapes.

Problem solving skills
Describing the properties carefully or using the properties to decide how to represent the shape.
Giving instructions to other children about where they should stand to make the shape.

Encouraging discussion
Ask children to talk about the shapes that they are drawing describing their properties to each other.

Links to prior experiences
What other 2-dimensional shapes can children see around the setting? What properties do they share?
What other 2-dimensional shapes can children on their walk or journey home from the setting? What properties do they share?

Possible misconceptions or difficulties
Careful use of language to help with pronunciation of words.

Subject knowledge for practitioners
Become confident in your own use of the vocabulary of shape. See page 000.

Personal and emotional development
Working together to give accurate instructions to each other.
Work as part of a group to discuss the properties of the shapes on their poster.

Activity 32: Ribbon shapes

Setting up the activity: Put a series of ribbons or thin strips of material in the centre of the table. There should also be digital cameras available if possible.

What to do:
Engage in free play with the children exploring the shapes that you can make with the ribbons. Make open and closed shapes and talk about the shapes that you make modelling the vocabulary of shape. When everyone round the table has made a shape talk about, "what is the same and what is different?" about the shapes.

Recording:
Take photographs of the shapes that are made. The children should select from these photographs for display. Create a poster which contains images of the shapes and is titled, "what is the same and what is different?"

What to ask:
What is the same and what is different about the shapes that you have drawn.
Can you make another shape that shares a property with that shape?
Tell me about your shape.

Words to use:
Use the mathematical names for the shapes.
Straight/curved edge.
Edges, vertices/corners.
Open/closed.

To develop the activity:
Use glue to attach some ribbon shapes to backing paper to create a poster.
Use pin-boards and elastic bands to create polygons.

Mathematical development

Age range	What a child is learning
Birth–11 months	Babies' early awareness of shape and space grows from their sensory awareness and opportunities to observe objects and their movements, and to play and explore.
8–20 months	Recognises shapes in meaningful contexts.
16–26 months	Attempts, sometimes successfully, to fit shapes into spaces on inset boards or jigsaw puzzles.
	Uses blocks to create their own simple structures and arrangements.
22–36 months	Beginning to categorise objects according to properties such as shape.
	Begins to use the language of shape.
30–50 months	Shows an interest in shape and space by playing with shapes or making arrangements with objects.
	Shows interest in shape by talking about shapes or arrangements.
	Uses shapes appropriately for tasks.
	Beginning to talk about the shapes of everyday objects, e.g. 'round' and 'tall'.
40–60+ months	Beginning to use mathematical names for 'solid' 3D shapes and 'flat' 2D shapes, and mathematical terms to describe shapes.

Active learning
Creating shapes and patterns using concrete materials engages the children actively in their learning and talking about properties of shape.

Problem solving skills
Exploring similarities and differences between the shapes.

Encouraging discussion
Talking about the properties of shapes and comparing them.
Selecting the shapes to use on the posters.

Links to prior experiences
What other 2-dimensional shapes can children see around the setting? What properties do they share?
What other 2-dimensional shapes can children on their walk or journey home from the setting? What properties do they share?

Possible misconceptions or difficulties
Careful use of language to help with pronunciation of words.

Subject knowledge for practitioners
Become confident in your own use of the vocabulary of shape. See page 000.

Personal and emotional development
Listening carefully to others describe their shapes.
Working together to select shapes for the posters.
Work as part of a group to discuss the properties of the shapes on their poster.

Activity 33: Building shapes

Setting up the activity: This activity takes place in the construction area. Children can use small building blocks inside or larger construction materials outside. A resource such as magnetic polydron (see resources) is ideal for this activity.

What to do:
Engage in free play with the children exploring the buildings you can make with the building blocks or construction materials. Talk about the shapes that you use whilst you are building modelling the vocabulary of shape. When everyone round the table has made a building talk about, "what is the same and what is different" about the shapes.

Recording:
Take photographs of the buildings that are made. The children should select from these photographs for display. Create a poster which contains photos of the buildings and is titled, "what is the same and what is different?"

What to ask:
What is the same and what is different about the buildings that you have drawn.
Can you make another building that shares a property with that shape?
Tell me about your building.

Words to use:
Use the mathematical names for the 3-dimensional shapes you are building with.
Straight/curved edge/face.
Edges, vertices/corners.

To develop the activity:
Create a story book using photographs of the buildings.
Use the buildings to create a housing estate or a tower block and describe it.

Mathematical development

Age range	What a child is learning
Birth–11 months	Babies' early awareness of shape and space grows from their sensory awareness and opportunities to observe objects and their movements, and to play and explore.
8–20 months	Recognises shapes in meaningful contexts.
16–26 months	Attempts, sometimes successfully, to fit shapes into spaces on inset boards or jigsaw puzzles. Uses blocks to create their own simple structures and arrangements.
22–36 months	Beginning to categorise objects according to properties such as shape. Begins to use the language of shape.
30–50 months	Shows an interest in shape and space by playing with shapes or making arrangements with objects. Shows awareness of similarities of shapes in the environment. Shows interest in shape by sustained construction activity or by talking about shapes or arrangements. Uses shapes appropriately for tasks. Beginning to talk about the shapes of everyday objects, e.g. 'round' and 'tall'.
40–60+ months	Beginning to use mathematical names for 'solid' 3D shapes and 'flat' 2D shapes, and mathematical terms to describe shapes. Selects a particular named shape. Uses familiar objects and common shapes to create and recreate patterns and build models.

Active learning
Using concrete materials to create constructions together actively engages the children in their learning and talking about properties of the shapes they are using.

Problem solving skills
Exploring similarities and differences between the 3-dimensional shapes and the constructions.

Encouraging discussion
Talking about the properties of the shapes, the buildings and comparing them.
Selecting the buildings that are best to use on the posters.

Links to prior experiences
What other 3-dimensional shapes can children see around the setting? What properties do they share?
What other 3-dimensional shapes can children on their walk or journey home from the setting? What properties do they share?

Possible misconceptions or difficulties
Careful use of language to help with pronunciation of words.

Subject knowledge for practitioners
Become confident in your own use of the vocabulary of shape. See page 000.

Personal and emotional development
Listening carefully to others describe their buildings.
Working together to select shapes for the posters.
Work as part of a group to discuss the properties of the buildings on their poster.

Activity 34: Shape treasure hunt

Setting up the activity: This can take place indoors or outdoors in any part of the school. You could even go to a local park or open space. You need to have visited the area so that you know that children will be able to find shapes with the appropriate properties.

What to do:
The children will work in teams. Each team should pick a person who will be the 'runner' and come to you with the shapes. Pick one of the group to act as a recorder for the game. Give a series of instructions. The teams should find a shape which has the properties you describe. They can either find the physical shape or point to it in the environment. For example:

* A 2-dimensional shape with straight edges.
* A 3-dimensional shape with a curved face.
* A 2-dimensional shape with curved edges.
* A 3-dimensional shape with more than 3 vertices.
* A 2-dimensional shape with 4 straight edges.
* A 3-dimensional shape with a square face.
* A 3-dimensional shape with a circular face.
* A cylinder.
* A rectangle.
* A cuboid.

Recording:
Children can take it in turns to record the scores. They should create their own system for this.

What to ask:
Show me that your shape has the properties.

Words to use:
Model the vocabulary of shape – see above.

To develop the activity:
The winning team can create a set of instructions for the next game.

Mathematical development

Age range	What a child is learning
Birth–11 months	Babies' early awareness of shape and space grows from their sensory awareness and opportunities to observe objects and their movements, and to play and explore.
8–20 months	Recognises shapes in meaningful contexts.
16–26 months	Attempts, sometimes successfully, to fit shapes into spaces on inset boards or jigsaw puzzles.
	Uses blocks to create their own simple structures and arrangements.
22–36 months	Notices simple shapes and patterns in pictures.
	Beginning to categorise objects according to properties such as shape.
	Begins to use the language of shape.
30–50 months	Shows an interest in shape and space by playing with shapes or making arrangements with objects.
	Shows awareness of similarities of shapes in the environment.
	Shows interest in shape by talking about shapes or arrangements.
	Shows interest in shapes in the environment.
	Uses shapes appropriately for tasks.
	Beginning to talk about the shapes of everyday objects, e.g. 'round' and 'tall'.
40–60+ months	Beginning to use mathematical names for 'solid' 3D shapes and 'flat' 2D shapes, and mathematical terms to describe shapes.
	Selects a particular named shape.

Active learning
Moving around the space to look for shapes with the given properties makes sure the children are engaged actively.

Problem solving skills
Checking that shapes have the given properties.
Finding alternative possibilities and checking other groups' shapes.

Encouraging discussion
Discussing the possible shapes which meet the requirements.
Checking that shapes which meet the requirements of the question.

Links to prior experiences
What other 2- and 3-dimensional shapes can children see around the setting? What properties do they share?
What other 2- and 3-dimensional shapes can children on their walk or journey home from the setting? What properties do they share?

Possible misconceptions or difficulties
Careful use of language to help with pronunciation of words.

Subject knowledge for practitioners
Become confident in your own use of the vocabulary of shape. See page 000.

Personal and emotional development
Listening carefully to others when finding the shapes that meet the requirements.
Working together to find shapes.
Work as part of a group to discuss the properties of shapes.

Activity 35: Shapes in pictures

Setting up the activity: Choose a series of abstract images, download images of artworks from the internet or use art books. Place these images in the centre of the table. This should take place in the creative area and all the art materials should be freely available.

What to do:
Engage in the art activity with the children. Look at the images on the table and talk about the shapes and the properties of the shapes that you can see.

Work with the children to create new images talking about the properties of the shapes as you paint or create.

Recording:
Use the images to create a display wall. Annotate the images with labels describing the properties of the shapes in the images.

What to ask:
What shapes can you see in that painting? What are the properties of the shapes?
What is the same and what is different about the paintings?
Tell me about your painting.

Words to use:
Use the mathematical names for the shapes in the images you are drawing.
Straight/curved edge.
Edges, vertices.

To develop the activity:
Visit an Art Gallery and explore the shapes within the pictures or ceramic designs at the Art Gallery.
Create a shape walk in the school for children to show to parents and carers.

Mathematical development

Age range	What a child is learning
Birth–11 months	Babies' early awareness of shape and space grows from their sensory awareness and opportunities to observe objects and their movements, and to play and explore.
8–20 months	Recognises shapes in meaningful contexts.
16–26 months	Attempts, sometimes successfully, to fit shapes into spaces on inset boards or jigsaw puzzles. Uses blocks to create their own simple structures and arrangements.
22–36 months	Notices simple shapes and patterns in pictures. Beginning to categorise objects according to properties such as shape. Begins to use the language of shape.
30–50 months	Shows an interest in shape and space by playing with shapes or making arrangements with objects. Shows awareness of similarities of shapes in the environment. Shows interest in shape by talking about shapes or arrangements. Shows interest in shapes in the environment. Uses shapes appropriately for tasks. Beginning to talk about the shapes of everyday objects, e.g. 'round' and 'tall'.
40–60+ months	Beginning to use mathematical names for 'solid' 3D shapes and 'flat' 2D shapes, and mathematical terms to describe shapes. Uses familiar objects and common shapes to create and recreate patterns and build models.

Active learning
Engaging in creative activity such as painting and talking about the process.

Problem solving skills
Planning the artwork based on looking at other pieces of art.
Accurately creating abstract pieces.

Encouraging discussion
Children should talk about the art work as they create their pieces.

Links to prior experiences
Have children visited art galleries – what sort of art do they like best?
Are their artworks, paintings or sculptures around the school or in/on other public build-ings? What shapes do they contain?

Possible misconceptions or difficulties
Careful use of language to help with pronunciation of words.

Subject knowledge for practitioners
Become confident in your own use of the vocabulary of shape. See page 000.

Personal and emotional development
Listening carefully to others when describing the artwork.
Work as part of a group to discuss the properties of shapes within the artworks.

8 | **Mainly measurement**

The activities in this section develop the following mathematical skills:

Age range	What a child is learning
Birth–11 months	Babies' early awareness of measure grows rom their sensory awareness and opportunities to play and explore.
8–20 months	Recognises big things and small things in meaningful contexts.
	Gets to know and enjoy daily routines, such as getting-up time, mealtimes, nappy time, and bedtime.
16–26 months	Enjoys filling and emptying containers.
	Associates a sequence of actions with daily routines.
	Beginning to understand that things might happen 'now'.
22–36 months	Beginning to categorise objects according to properties such as shape or size.
	Begins to use the language of size.
	Understands some talk about immediate past and future, e.g. 'before', 'later' or 'soon'.
	Anticipates specific time-based events such as mealtimes or home time.
30–50 months	Uses positional language.
40–60+ months	Can describe their relative position such as 'behind' or 'next to'.
	Orders two or three items by length or height.
	Orders two items by weight or capacity.
	Uses everyday language related to time.
	Beginning to use everyday language related to money.
	Orders and sequences familiar events.
	Measures short periods of time in simple ways.

Remember, children develop at their own rates, and in their own ways. These statements and their order should not be taken as necessary steps or checklists for individual children.

By the end of Year 1 children should:

- choose and use appropriate standard units to estimate and measure length/height in any direction (m/cm); mass (kg/g); temperature (°C); capacity (litres/ml) to the nearest appropriate unit, using rulers, scales, thermometers and measuring vessels; compare and order lengths, mass, volume/capacity and record the results using >, < and =.

* recognise and use symbols for pounds (£) and pence (p); combine amounts to make a particular value; find different combinations of coins that equal the same amounts of money; solve simple problems in a practical context involving addition and sub-traction of money of the same unit, including giving change.

* compare and sequence intervals of time; tell and write the time to five minutes, including quarter past/to the hour and draw the hands on a clock face to show these times; know the number of minutes in an hour and the number of hours in a day.

Routine activities: There should be opportunities to estimate, measure and compare as part of day-to day activities moving from using non-standard units such as cubes or hands to standard units. Similarly, money should be available throughout the year for role-play activities. Make sure there are clocks around the setting, both analogue and digital and refer to the time every-day, throughout the day.

Activity 36: Designing clothes

Setting up the activity: You will need a variety of small pieces of fabrics or coloured paper and tissue paper and small dolls or other toys, animals for example. They will also need scissors and adhesive tape.

What to do:
Talk about the clothes that the children are wearing. How do they know that they fit? How do they choose clothes or do adults choose for them? If they could choose their own clothes what would they wear? If they could design their own clothes what would they look like? Encourage children to design some clothes that they would like to wear.

They should then use the fabric or tissue paper to design and make clothes for the dolls or toy animals. They should make sure they fit by comparing the lengths of the pieces of fabric with the lengths of the dolls or animals.

Recording:
Take photographs of this activity and ask the children to select their favourite photographs for display.

What to ask:
Tell me about your design? What size will it be?
How do you know that will fit your doll?
Should it be bigger/smaller/longer/shorter?

Words to use:
Longer; shorter, wider, thinner, bigger, smaller.
How big/small?
What size?

To develop the activity:
Visit a local clothes factory or shop or even ask a local fashion designer or a parent who is skilled in making clothes to come into the setting and work with the children.

Mathematical development

Age range	What a child is learning
Birth–11 months	Babies' early awareness of measure grows rom their sensory awareness and opportunities to play and explore.
8–20 months	Recognises big things and small things in meaningful contexts.
16–26 months	Beginning to understand that things might happen 'now'.
22–36 months	Beginning to categorise objects according to properties such as shape or size.
	Begins to use the language of size.
30–50 months	Uses positional language.
40–60+ months	Orders two or three items by length or height.

Active learning
Being creative in designing their own clothes and making clothes for animals or dolls engages the children actively.

Problem solving skills
Explaining the designs that they like and planning and creating these designs.
Making sure that clothes are the right size for animals or dolls.

Encouraging discussion
Children should be encouraged to talk about the designs they are working on as they create the designs.
They can check each other's clothes to make sure that they fit the dolls and animals.

Links to prior experiences
Ask if the children's parents/carers make their own clothes.
Where do they buy their clothes?
Where do they think their clothes are made?

Possible misconceptions or difficulties
Not taking care with comparisons – model how to make sure that you hold the clothes against the dolls and animals to make accurate comparisons.

Subject knowledge for practitioners
The measurement should be through comparison at this stage. It would be inappropriate and not efficient to use standard units.

Personal and emotional development
Sharing and commenting on each other's designs and speak about their ideas
Being sensitive to others' ideas and drawing on these ideas to develop designs
Working as part of a group.
Talking about traditional dress from a range of cultures.

Activity 37: Pets' homes

Setting up the activity: Find a story book about homes for animals. There will be lots to choose from. It may not be appropriate to use *Three Little Pigs* for cultural reasons. An alternative would be non-fiction books on zoos or looking after animals. You may also be able to find a video about keeping small animals in cages or about a zoo. You will also need lots of modelling materials and equipment. You could also work outside and create dens or larger 'houses' for larger animals.

What to do:
Read the book or watch the video as an inspiration and then allow the children to choose which animal they want to make a house for. They should make a plan for the house and explain what it will look and then use the modelling equipment to make and decorate the house

Recording:
The children should draw a plan of what they want the house to look like and then take photographs of the finished houses.

What to ask:
Tell me about your design? What size will it be?
How do you know that will fit your animal?
Should it be bigger/smaller/longer/shorter/higher/lower?
Is there enough space? How do you know?

Words to use:
Longer, shorter, wider, thinner, bigger, smaller, higher, lower, taller.
How big/small?
What size?

To develop the activity:
Visit a local pet shop or zoo and look at the cages and kennels and so on.

Mathematical development

Age range	What a child is learning
Birth–11 months	Babies' early awareness of measure grows rom their sensory awareness and opportunities to play and explore.
8–20 months	Recognises big things and small things in meaningful contexts.
16–26 months	Beginning to understand that things might happen 'now'.
22–36 months	Beginning to categorise objects according to properties such as shape or size. Begins to use the language of size.
30–50 months	Uses positional language.
40–60+ months	Orders two or three items by length or height.

Active learning
Being creative in designing and making the houses for animals engages the children actively.

Problem solving skills
Explaining the designs and then planning and creating the houses from their ideas.
Making sure that houses are the right size for the animals and being able to explain how they know.

Encouraging discussion
Children should be encouraged to talk about the designs they are working on as they create the houses.
They can talk about and evaluate each other's houses to make sure that they are suitable for the animals.

Links to prior experiences
Ask if the children's parents/carers can make houses or other constructions.
Do they have pets? Have they got a 'house'?

Possible misconceptions or difficulties
Not taking care with comparisons – model how to make sure that you use the animals to make accurate comparisons and to check that the house is the appropriate size.

Subject knowledge for practitioners
The measurement should be through comparison at this stage. It would be inappropriate and not efficient to use standard units.

Personal and emotional development
Sharing and commenting on each other's designs and speak about their ideas.
Being sensitive to others' ideas and drawing on these ideas to develop the designs.
Working as part of a group to create the houses.

Activity 38: Filling buckets

Setting up the activity: Use the water play area outside. This is also great fun if you are on a visit to the seaside or a play area with a paddling pool. Have a variety of buckets and other containers. The more the better and lots of different shapes and sizes.

What to do:
Model filling up a small container and pouring it into a larger container with the children. Count the number of times it takes you to fill the larger container from the smaller container. Then try different sized containers

Recording:
The children should record the results of their investigations in any way they want to. Ask them to explain what their marks mean at the end of the session.

What to ask:
How many times?
Is that container bigger/smaller?
Does it hold more/less?
Which do you think holds most? Try it out.

Words to use:
Full/half full/ empty.
How many times.
How high.
How far up the container?
Water level.

To develop the activity:
Children can predict how far up the water will come and mark with a line before they test out their estimation.

Mathematical development

Age range	What a child is learning
Birth–11 months	Babies' early awareness of measure grows rom their sensory awareness and opportunities to play and explore.
8–20 months	Recognises big things and small things in meaningful contexts.
16–26 months	Enjoys filling and emptying containers.
22–36 months	Beginning to categorise objects according to properties such as shape or size.
	Begins to use the language of size.
30–50 months	Uses positional language.
40–60+ months	Orders two items by weight or capacity.

Active learning
Children love pouring water from one container to another. This activity uses this motivation to help them come to understand capacity in an active way.

Problem solving skills
Making predictions and testing them out
Ordering containers by capacity – carrying out an investigation to do this.

Encouraging discussion
Children should be encouraged to discuss their predictions throughout the activity. Model this by being explicit about your own thinking as you engage with them.

Links to prior experiences
What containers do they use every-day? Water bottles; juice bottles and so on. Which do they think hold the most liquid?
What containers do they know are used at home? Which hold the most?

Possible misconceptions or difficulties
Not filling the containers to the top to make comparisons. Model how to accurately fill a container.

Subject knowledge for practitioners
This activity explores conservation of measures – see page 000 in Section 1.

Personal and emotional development
Cooperating and taking turns with the filling of containers.
Speak about their ideas and predictions – testing them out together.
Working as part of a group.

Activity 39: Pets at the swimming pool

Setting up the activity: You need some beach towels for comparison and then pieces of fabric or paper or card that can be used to design and make beach towels for dolls or toy animals.

What to do:
Show the children the beach towels. You could set the role play area up as a beach or a swimming pool. The children should explore the beach towels so that get used to the relative size of the towels to their bodies.

Children use the material or paper to design and make towels that are an appropriate size for the dolls or the animals.

Recording:
Take a photograph of the finished towels with the toys at the beach or create a story book about a trip to the swimming pool using the towels.

What to ask:
Tell me about your design? What size will the towel be?
How do you know that will fit your animal/doll?
Should it be bigger/smaller/longer/shorter?

Words to use:
Longer, shorter, wider, thinner, bigger, smaller.
How big/small?
What size?

To develop the activity:
Design other items for the role play area – swimming googles, fins for the dolls feet and so on.

Mathematical development

Age range	What a child is learning
Birth–11 months	Babies' early awareness of measure grows rom their sensory awareness and opportunities to play and explore.
8–20 months	Recognises big things and small things in meaningful contexts.
16–26 months	Beginning to understand that things might happen 'now'.
22–36 months	Beginning to categorise objects according to properties such as shape or size.
	Begins to use the language of size.
30–50 months	Uses positional language.
40–60+ months	Orders two or three items by length or height.

Active learning
Being creative in designing and making the towels for the dolls/animals and creating/ telling a story engages the children actively.

Problem solving skills
Explaining the designs and then planning and creating the towels from their ideas.
Making sure that the towels are the right size for the animals and being able to explain how they know they are the right size.

Encouraging discussion
Children should be encouraged to talk about the designs they are working on as they create the towels.
They can talk about and evaluate each other's towels to make sure that they are suitable for the animals.

Links to prior experiences
Do they go to the swimming pool?
How big are the towels that they take?
Are they bigger or smaller than towels at bath-time?

Possible misconceptions or difficulties
Not taking care with comparisons – model how to make sure that you use the animals to make accurate comparisons and to check that the towel is the appropriate size.

Subject knowledge for practitioners
The measurement should be through comparison at this stage. It would be inappropriate and not efficient to use standard units.

Personal and emotional development
Sharing and commenting on each other's designs and speak about their ideas.
Being sensitive to others' ideas and drawing on these ideas to develop the designs.
Working as part of a group to create the towels and to create the story.

Activity 40: Day and night

Setting up the activity: Find two stories. One that happens in the day and one that happens at night. *Slinky Malinki* in the *Hairy Maclary* series is set at night. The rest of the series are all set in the day time. Download images from the web of things that happen in the day and things that happen at night.

What to do:
In circle time talk about day and night. How can we tell whether it is daytime or night time? What do we do in the day? What do we do at night? Read the stories together as a whole group. Tell the children that they are going to make up their own stories about the daytime and the night time. They can either use the pictures that you have cut out as their illustrations or they can make their own illustrations.

Recording:
It is important that the children use emergent writing to create the stories. They should then tell you the story and you can write the story underneath the emergent writing so that the stories can be shared with the parents and carers.

What to ask:
What happens in the day time?
What happens at night time?
How do you know it is the day?
How do you know it is the night?

Words to use:
Day/night.
Before/afterwards.
How long?

To develop the activity:
Develop the activity to include morning/afternoon/evening.

Mathematical development

Age range	What a child is learning
Birth–11 months	Babies' early awareness of measure grows rom their sensory awareness and opportunities to play and explore.
8–20 months	Gets to know and enjoy daily routines, such as getting-up time, mealtimes, nappy time, and bedtime.
16–26 months	Associates a sequence of actions with daily routines. Beginning to understand that things might happen 'now'.
22–36 months	Understands some talk about immediate past and future, e.g. 'before', 'later' or 'soon'. Anticipates specific time-based events such as mealtimes or home time.
30–50 months	Uses positional language.
40–60+ months	Uses everyday language related to time. Orders and sequences familiar events. Measures short periods of time in simple ways.

Active learning
Engaging creatively in telling and recording a story develops children's understanding of time in an active way.

Problem solving skills
Explaining the difference between night and day.
Listening to peers explain what they do in the day and at night and comparing it with their own experience.

Encouraging discussion
Encourage children to talk in pairs and small groups about their own experiences.
The children should construct the story together through discussion.

Links to prior experiences
The whole activity is located in the experience of the children.

Possible misconceptions or difficulties
Day and night might be linked to light and dark at this stage. This becomes confusing when you go to bed and it is still light.

Subject knowledge for practitioners
Being sensitive to different routines at home. Avoid being judgemental.

Personal and emotional development
Planning and creating together.
Speaking about their ideas and listening carefully to others.
Working as part of a group.

Activity 41: How many jumps?

Setting up the activity: Collect a range of egg timers. They should include a one-minute timer.

What to do:
Let the children explore the timers in free play. What do they notice about the different timers? How do they think they work? Talk about the types of things that you can time. Suggest:

- Jumping up and down.
- Throwing and catching a ball.
- Writing your name.
- Rolling a 2 on a dice.
- Saying, "hello".

Take other suggestions from the children. Tell them they are going to use the one-minute timer to see how many times they can do an activity in one-minute.

Recording:
The children should devise a way of recording each activity and how many times in a minute different children can carry out that activity.

What to ask:
How long?
How long left?
How many times?

Words to use:
1/2/3 minute(s).
How long?

To develop the activity:
Use the other timers and use timers on tablets or the smart board to time activities. This can be an every-day event. For example, set a timer for tidying up.

Mathematical development

Age range	What a child is learning
Birth–11 months	Babies' early awareness of measure grows from their sensory awareness and opportunities to play and explore.
8–20 months	Gets to know and enjoy daily routines, such as getting-up time, mealtimes, nappy time, and bedtime.
16–26 months	Associates a sequence of actions with daily routines. Beginning to understand that things might happen 'now'.
22–36 months	Understands some talk about immediate past and future, e.g. 'before', 'later' or 'soon'. Anticipates specific time-based events such as mealtimes or home time.
30–50 months	Uses positional language.
40–60+ months	Orders and sequences familiar events. Measures short periods of time in simple ways.

Active learning
Timing activities allows children to relate the passing of time to the number of times they can carry out an activity.

Problem solving skills
Estimating time.
Making estimations and evaluating how accurate their estimate was.

Encouraging discussion
Pupils should discuss the sorts of activities they can time.
Pupils should discuss their estimates of how many times they think they can carry out an activity in one minute.

Links to prior experiences
What is timed at home (cooking?)
Some children may be given time limits for using tablets or watching TV.

Possible misconceptions or difficulties
Children might measure time in 'number of jumps' rather than using the time assuming it takes everyone the same time to jump 20 times for example.

Subject knowledge for practitioners
Use the language of time, that is seconds and minutes even though full understanding will come at a later stage.

Personal and emotional development
Planning activities together to decide what they will time.
Taking it in turns to be the 'timer'.
Working as part of a group.

Activity 42: Fishing

Setting up the activity: Make a set of different sized fish. These should be laminated and placed in a box to represent a pool. Make some small 'nets' to use to play fishing. Alternatively use toy fish in the water-play area outside and a real fishing net.

What to do:
Set up the fishing game on a table or in the role-play area. Have a box of cubes on the table.

The children take it in turns to catch the fish and lay out the fish in front of them when they catch one. When they finish 'fishing' they compare the fish. Ask them to compare the fish by placing the next to each other at first. Then model how to use the cubes to measure the lengths of the fish.

Recording:
Children should devise a way of recording the different lengths of the fish and which children have caught which fish.

What to ask:
Who caught the longest fish?
Who caught the shortest fish? How do you know?

Words to use:
How long?
Longest/shortest.
How many cubes long?

To develop the activity:
Children can answer questions such as "how much longer is that fish?"

Mathematical development

Age range	What a child is learning
Birth–11 months	Babies' early awareness of measure grows rom their sensory awareness and opportunities to play and explore.
8–20 months	Recognises big things and small things in meaningful contexts.
16–26 months	Enjoys filling and emptying containers. Associates a sequence of actions with daily routines. Beginning to understand that things might happen 'now'.
22–36 months	Beginning to categorise objects according to properties such as shape or size. Begins to use the language of size.
30–50 months	Uses positional language.
40–60+ months	Can describe their relative position such as 'behind' or 'next to'. Orders two or three items by length or height.

Active learning
Playing the game and catching the fish provides the motivation for wanting to measure the fish and compare them.

Problem solving skills
Agreeing how to compare the fish.
Comparing results.
Ordering fish by length.

Encouraging discussion
Children should talk about the fish they have caught and predict who has the longest fish before they measure them.
Children should discuss how best to record the activity.

Links to prior experiences
Ask children if their parents or carers go fishing
Where do they see fish?
What is the biggest fish they know?
Visit a fishmonger's shop or a market stall.

Possible misconceptions or difficulties
Not lining up the fish so that the 'tails' start in a line. Model this to the children.

Subject knowledge for practitioners
This activity explores conservation of length as well as introducing measurement in standard units.

Personal and emotional development
Cooperating and taking turns in catching fish.
Working as a group to measure the fish.

Activity 43: My day

Setting up the activity: Cut out a series of images that can be sequenced, For example, someone waking up; getting dressed; going to school; eating lunch and so on. Find a story which takes place over a day with events in sequence.

What to do:
Read the story together as a whole group. Ask children to predict what will happen on the next page. Make silly suggestions like, "Will she put her pyjamas back on?" in the morning.

Tell the children that they are going to make up their own stories about their favourite ever day. They can either use the pictures that you have cut out as their illustrations or they can make their own illustrations.

Recording:
It is important that the children use emergent writing to create the stories. They should then tell you the story and you can write the story underneath the emergent writing so that the stories can be shared with the parents and carers.

What to ask:
What happens first in your story?
What will happen next?
What happens at the end of the day?

Words to use:
Morning.
Dinner time/lunch time.
Afternoon.
Tea time.
Night time.

To develop the activity:
Develop the activity to include different events on different days.

Mathematical development

Age range	What a child is learning
Birth–11 months	Babies' early awareness of measure grows rom their sensory awareness and opportunities to play and explore.
8–20 months	Gets to know and enjoy daily routines, such as getting-up time, mealtimes, nappy time, and bedtime.
16–26 months	Associates a sequence of actions with daily routines. Beginning to understand that things might happen 'now'.
22–36 months	Understands some talk about immediate past and future, e.g. 'before', 'later' or 'soon'. Anticipates specific time-based events such as mealtimes or home time.
30–50 months	Uses positional language.
40–60+ months	Uses everyday language related to time. Orders and sequences familiar events. Measures short periods of time in simple ways.

Active learning
Engaging creatively in telling and recording a story develops children understanding of time in an active way.

Problem solving skills
Explaining the how they understand the chronology of events.
   Listening to peers explain what they do during the day comparing it with their own experience.

Encouraging discussion
Encourage children to talk in pairs and small groups about their own experiences.
The children should construct the story together through discussion.

Links to prior experiences
The whole activity is located in the experience of the children.

Possible misconceptions or difficulties
Chronology will be much clearer than the time that things take place.

Subject knowledge for practitioners
Begin to introduce the times of day to model vocabulary rather than to expect understanding at this stage.

Personal and emotional development
Planning and creating the together.
Speaking about their ideas and listening carefully to others.
Working as part of a group.

Activity 44: Making dens

Setting up the activity: This is an outdoor activity and perfect for a school trip or visit. It would make a perfect Forest School activity. You need a range of sticks or garden canes and large pieces of material or waterproof groundsheets to provide cover. You will also need adhesive tape which is strong enough to attach the material to the sticks.

What to do:
The children will work in small groups to create their own dens. They should be big enough to hold 4 people. You can set other criteria, for example the children should be able to stand up or lie down or all sit in a circle to eat.

When the children have finished making the dens they should look at each other's and decide which they like best and why.

Recording:
Take photographs of the dens to create a display in the setting and share the learning with parents and carers.

What to ask:
Tell me about your den? How big will it be?
How do you know that will fit your group?
Should it be bigger/smaller/longer/shorter/higher/lower/wider?
Is there enough space? How do you know?

Words to use:
Longer, shorter, wider, thinner, bigger, smaller, higher, lower, taller.
How big/small.
What size?

To develop the activity:
Have den making equipment in the role-play area so that the activity can be repeated throughout the year.

Visit a construction site or ask a parent or carer who is involved in construction to visit the setting.

Mathematical development

Age range	What a child is learning
Birth–11 months	Babies' early awareness of measure grows rom their sensory awareness and opportunities to play and explore.
8–20 months	Recognises big things and small things in meaningful contexts.
16–26 months	Beginning to understand that things might happen 'now'.
22–36 months	Beginning to categorise objects according to properties such as shape or size.
	Begins to use the language of size.
30–50 months	Uses positional language.
40–60+ months	Orders two or three items by length or height.

Active learning
Being creative in designing and making the dens engages the children actively.

Problem solving skills
Explaining the planning and creating the dens from their ideas.

Making sure that dens are the right size and meet the criteria you have set and being able to explain how they know.

Encouraging discussion
Children should be encouraged to talk about the designs they are working on as they create the dens.

They can talk about and evaluate each other's dens to make sure that they meet the criteria.

Links to prior experiences
Ask if the children's parents/carers can make houses or other constructions.
Where have they seen construction sites.

Possible misconceptions or difficulties
Not taking care with comparisons – model how to make sure you make accurate comparisons to check that the den is the appropriate size and meets the criteria.

Subject knowledge for practitioners
The measurement should be through comparison at this stage. It would be inappropriate and not efficient to use standard units.

Personal and emotional development
Sharing and commenting on each other's designs and speak about their ideas.
Being sensitive to others' ideas and drawing on these ideas to develop the designs.
Working as part of a group to create the dens.

Activity 45: Big and small walk

Setting up the activity: You need a range of sizes of boxes. They all need to be able to carried by a child but should range from very small to quite large. There should be enough boxes so that each group of children can use 3 or 4 of them. This activity needs to take place in a park or a woodland. It is an ideal Forest School activity.

What to do:
The children go on a walk and find objects that fit in their boxes, they should fit tightly into the box so that they have approximately the same dimensions. As the children collect the objects use the vocabulary of measurement to compare the measurements.

Recording:
Take a collection of the objects back to the classroom and put them on a display table. Label the objects using the vocabulary of measurement. The children should decide on the labels. For example, "long, medium-sized, short". "Smaller than my finger; longer than my finger."

What to ask:
What is the longest/shortest object?
What is the widest/thinnest object?
What is the heaviest/lightest object?

Words to use:
How long/wide/heavy?
Longest/shortest/lightest/heaviest.
How many cubes long?

To develop the activity:
Children can start to compare objects using standard units.

Mathematical development

Age range	What a child is learning
Birth–11 months	Babies' early awareness of measure grows from their sensory awareness and opportunities to play and explore.
8–20 months	Recognises big things and small things in meaningful contexts.
16–26 months	Enjoys filling and emptying containers.
22–36 months	Beginning to categorise objects according to properties such as shape or size. Begins to use the language of size.
30–50 months	Uses positional language.
40–60+ months	Can describe their relative position such as 'behind' or 'next to'. Orders two or three items by length or height. Orders two items by weight or capacity.

Active learning
Finding objects that fit in the containers provides the motivation for wanting to measure the objects and compare them.

Problem solving skills
Agreeing how to compare the objects.
Comparing results with other groups.
Ordering by length and weight.

Encouraging discussion
Children should talk about the objects they have collected and predict who has the longest/heaviest objects before they compare them.
Children should discuss how best to label the objects on the table.

Links to prior experiences
What long/short things do they have at home?
What do they think is the heaviest object in the classroom?

Possible misconceptions or difficulties
Not lining up the objects accurately to compare the lengths. Model this to the children.

Subject knowledge for practitioners
This activity explores conservation of measures as well as introducing measurement in standard units.

Personal and emotional development
Cooperating and working together to collect the objects.
Working as a group to compare the objects and create the display.

9 | Mainly algebra

Whilst the English National Curriculum and the Early Learning Goals do not explicitly state objectives for algebra, Chapter 1 in Section 1 explained why I feel it is important that we view children in the early years as capable of developing their algebraic understandings. As I stated in Chapter 1 the Primary years Programme (PYP) of the International Baccalaureate does explicitly offer objectives for algebra, under the heading 'Pattern and function' for phase 1 of the curriculum. This objective is:

> Learners will understand that patterns and sequences occur in everyday situations. They will be able to identify, describe, extend and create patterns in various ways.

This matches the statement in Early Learning Goal 12 that, "Children . . . recognise, create and describe patterns." It also supports children in moving towards an understanding of, "patterns in the number system (for example odd and even numbers)" and in developing the ability to, "recognise and create repeating patterns with objects and shapes", which are expectations by the end of the first year of primary school. Below is a table adapted from *Development Matters* which outlines experiences I would describe as early algebra.

Age range	What a child is learning
Birth–11 months	Notices changes in number of objects/images or sounds in group of up to 3.
8–20 months	Recognises shapes in meaningful contexts.
16–26 months	Knows that things exist, even when out of sight. Beginning to organise and categorise objects

Age range	What a child is learning
22–36 months	Recites some number names in sequence. Creates and experiments with symbols and marks representing ideas of number. Beginning to categorise objects according to properties such as shape or size. Notices simple shapes and patterns in pictures.
30–50 months	Uses some number names and number language spontaneously. Uses some number names accurately in play. Beginning to represent numbers using fingers, marks on paper or pictures. Compares two groups of objects, saying when they have the same number. Separates a group of three or four objects in different ways, beginning to recognise that the total is still the same. Shows interest in shape by sustained construction activity or by talking about shapes or arrangements.
40–60+ months	In practical activities and discussion, beginning to use the vocabulary involved in adding and subtracting. Records, using marks that they can interpret and explain. Begins to identify own mathematical problems based on own interests and fascinations. Orders two or three items by length, height, weight or capacity. Uses familiar objects and common shapes to create and recreate patterns and build models.

Remember, children develop at their own rates, and in their own ways. These statements and their order should not be taken as necessary steps or checklists for individual children.

Routine activities

Look out for repeating patterns both in numbers and in shapes. Jewellery or fabrics often contain patterns that can be discussed. You will also notice number patterns in house numbers whenever you go out for a walk with the children.

You can create patterns using the children whenever they are queuing using colours of items of clothing. You can ask children to line up "Red, blue, red, blue and so on."

Activity 46: Necklaces

Setting up the activity: You need materials for making necklaces. This may include strings for threading beads or buttons or pasta onto. You could also use wool or string. It is also helpful to bring in examples of necklaces which are made by repeating patterns of beads. You may want to put different colours or shapes into different pots for younger children. Alternatively, the activity can begin with the children sorting the objects into those with similar properties themselves.

What to do:
Sit at the table with the children and begin to make a necklace yourself modelling the process to the children. Start with a simple repeating pattern such as red, blue, red, blue or square, triangle, square, triangle and ask the children what they notice. Develop the complexity of the patterns so that there may be two red beads followed by one yellow bead and then one blue bead.

The children should then create their own patterns and talk about them.

Recording:
Take photographs of the finished necklaces or glue them onto backing paper to use as a display. Ask the children to describe the patterns to you and write down their descriptions. The children can also record the patterns in any way that they choose.

What to ask:
What do you notice?
What could come next? Why do you say that?
Tell me about your pattern.

Words to use:
Repeating pattern.

To develop the activity:
Children can design increasingly complex patterns.
Children can describe each other's patterns.

Mathematical development

Age range	What a child is learning
Birth–11 months	Notices changes in number of objects/images or sounds in group of up to 3.
8–20 months	Recognises shapes in meaningful contexts.
16–26 months	Beginning to organise and categorise objects
22–36 months	Beginning to categorise objects according to properties such as shape or size.
	Notices simple shapes and patterns in pictures.
30–50 months	Shows interest in shape by sustained construction activity or by talking about shapes or arrangements.
40–60+ months	Records, using marks that they can interpret and explain.
	Uses familiar objects and common shapes to create and recreate patterns and build models.

Active learning
Creating, designing and describing the necklaces and talking about the patterns engages the children actively in their learning.

Problem solving skills
Designing repeating patterns.
Talking about repeating patterns and noticing when patterns do not repeat.
Discussing others patterns and suggesting alternatives.

Encouraging discussion
The children should talk about the patterns that you are making and discuss the possible patterns they can make as well as describing the patterns that they are making.

Links to prior experiences
Children could bring examples of necklaces in from home.
Parents or carers may be jewellery designers and could come into the setting to work with the children.

Possible misconceptions or difficulties
Children may not possess the fine motor skills to make the necklaces – you can work with them threading the items they choose onto the strings.

Subject knowledge for practitioners
Allow the children to describe the patterns that they are making. They may be thinking of a pattern that you have not noticed.

Personal and emotional development
Planning the activity together and talking about the necklaces that each other are making.
Being sensitive to others and appreciating all the designs.
Working as part of a group.
Different cultural groups may have particular significance for necklaces.

Activity 47: Wallpaper designs

Setting up the activity: Bring in a selection of wallpaper designs (or fabrics) which contain repeating patterns. You will also need printing blocks and paints to create repeating patterns as well as a large roll of paper to use to create the wallpaper.

What to do:
Give pairs of children a piece of wallpaper or fabric. Ask them to describe the pattern to the other children. They should describe what repeats – is it shapes, colours or both. Do the images repeat next to each other? Up and down? Both?

The children should then create their own patterns using the equipment that you have provided and talk about the designs.

Recording:
Take photographs of the finished designs or use them as a display. Ask the children to describe the designs to you and write down their descriptions. The children can also record the designs in any way that they choose.

What to ask:
What do you notice?
What will repeat in your design?
Where will the next object go?
Tell me about your design.

Words to use:
Repeating pattern.

To develop the activity:
Children can develop increasingly complex designs.
Children can describe each other's designs and describe designs they see around school.
Children can take photographs of designs at home and describe them.

Mathematical development

Age range	What a child is learning
Birth–11 months	Notices changes in number of objects/images or sounds in group of up to 3.
8–20 months	Recognises shapes in meaningful contexts.
16–26 months	Beginning to organise and categorise objects
22–36 months	Beginning to categorise objects according to properties such as shape or size. Notices simple shapes and patterns in pictures.
30–50 months	Shows interest in shape by sustained construction activity or by talking about shapes or arrangements.
40–60+ months	Records, using marks that they can interpret and explain. Uses familiar objects and common shapes to create and recreate patterns and build models.

Active learning
Designing and creating the wallpaper and talking about the patterns engages the children actively in their learning and thinking.

Problem solving skills
Designing repeating patterns.
Talking about repeating patterns in their designs and noticing when patterns do not repeat.
Discussing others' designs and suggesting improvements and alternatives.

Encouraging discussion
The children should talk about the designs they are making and describe the repeating patterns in other children's designs.

Links to prior experiences
Take photographs of your wallpaper at home and invite parents and carers to do the same.
Look for repeating patterns around the school.

Possible misconceptions or difficulties
Children may not possess the fine motor skills to work accurately– you can work with them to support them but allow children to create for themselves. It is noticing repeating patterns that is important at this stage.

Subject knowledge for practitioners
Allow the children to describe the designs that they are making. They may be thinking of a pattern that you have not noticed.

Personal and emotional development
Planning the designs together and talking about the designs that each other are making.
Being sensitive to others and appreciating all the designs that are being created.
Working as part of a group.

Activity 48: Lining up

Setting up the activity: This activity does not need any resources except for the children. They can repeat the activity using dolls or figures or vehicles.

What to do:
Ask three children to come to the front. They should line up in any way they like. The children talk about the line. The children then line up in a different way. Ask the same questions. Add another person to the line and ask the questions again.

Recording:
If the children play with figures or objects take photographs.
They can describe their lines – and ask the children to write about the line using emergent writing.
Write down their descriptions under there emergent writing.

What to ask:
Who is first?
Who is in the middle?
Who is at the end?
Who is in between?

Words to use:
Front; back, in-between, middle.
First, second, third, fourth and so on.

To develop the activity:
Ask children with different coloured tops to line up to create a pattern or line up boy, girl, boy, girl so there is a repeating pattern.

Mathematical development

Age range	What a child is learning
Birth–11 months	Notices changes in number of objects/images or sounds in group of up to 3.
8–20 months	Recognises shapes in meaningful contexts.
16–26 months	Beginning to organise and categorise objects
22–36 months	Creates and experiments with symbols and marks. Beginning to categorise objects according to properties. Notices simple patterns.
30–50 months	Beginning to represent using fingers, marks on paper or pictures. Compares two groups of objects. Separates a group of three or four objects in different ways, beginning to recognise that the total is still the same. Shows interest in shape by sustained construction activity or by talking about arrangements.
40–60+ months	Records, using marks that they can interpret and explain. Begins to identify own mathematical problems based on own interests and fascinations. Orders two or three items. Uses familiar objects and common shapes to create and recreate patterns and build models.

Active learning
Involve as many of the children as you can in making the lines to engage them all in the activity actively.
Moving figures or objects into different arrangements engages the children actively.

Problem solving skills
Finding different arrangements and describing them.
Finding alternative arrangements.
Finding as many arrangements as they can.

Encouraging discussion
Whole group discussion about describing the line and finding alternative arrangements.
Talking about their own arrangements of objects.

Links to prior experiences
When do they have to stand in line?
How do they decide who goes first who and who is at the end?

Possible misconceptions or difficulties
Using the different words for the same position. For example, first and front or third, at the back, last.

Subject knowledge for practitioners
Use a range of vocabulary and repeat the activity as a day-to-day part of classroom routines so that children become familiar with the language.

Personal and emotional development
Cooperating and taking turns. Being happy to be first or last in a line.
Planning different arrangements together and speaking about their ideas.

Activity 49: Teddy bears' picnic

Setting up the activity: You need cups and saucers and plates and play food. This can either be made using modelling resources or you can buy play food. Include a range of food. This activity can remain in the role-play area.

What to do:
With the children set out a picnic blanket. The children should place the teddy bears around the blanket. Check that they are, "not too close together". Children should give each teddy bear a plate and a cup and saucer and eating utensils. They may choose to give the bigger teddy bears the larger cups and saucers. Talk about the decisions they are making. Share out the food so that each bear has a "fair share".

Recording
Take photographs of the activity and ask the children to talk about the image. Write down their observations underneath the image.

What to ask
How many plates?
Has everyone got a plate/cup/saucer?
What is missing?

Words to use
How many?
How many left?
Fair.

To develop the activity:
Children can plan and make their own picnic for a school trip.

Mathematical development

Age range	What a child is learning
Birth–11 months	Notices changes in number of objects/images or sounds in group of up to 3.
8–20 months	Recognises shapes in meaningful contexts.
16–26 months	Knows that things exist, even when out of sight. Beginning to organise and categorise objects
22–36 months	Beginning to categorise objects according to properties such as shape or size. Notices simple shapes and patterns in pictures.
30–50 months	Uses some number names and number language spontaneously. Uses some number names accurately in play. Beginning to represent numbers using fingers, marks on paper or pictures. Compares two groups of objects, saying when they have the same number.
40–60+ months	Begins to identify own mathematical problems based on own interests and fascinations. Uses familiar objects and common shapes to create and recreate patterns.

Active learning
The children should all take part in setting up the picnic. Take it in turns to try out different arrangements so that all the children have experience in setting out the picnic.

Problem solving skills
Checking each bear has one of everything.
Noticing what is missing.
Finding alternative ways to share out the food and the cups, saucers and plates.

Encouraging discussion
Children should talk about the decisions they are making and the possible alternatives.

Links to prior experiences
School trips that they have been on that involved a picnic or a shared meal.
Shared meals at home – what are family traditions for meal times?
School dinner times – what are the routines?

Possible misconceptions or difficulties
This may be something that is outside the children's experience. Model it by using a story or a piece of video.

Subject knowledge for practitioners
There may be different family routines that you should be aware of. Some children may eat alone, some families will all eat together sitting on the floor. Different cultural backgrounds will use different eating utensils.

Personal and emotional development
Cooperating and taking turns to set up the picnic.
Being sensitive to others home routines and diets.
Working as part of a group.

Activity 50: Bucket balances

Setting up the activity: You need a set of bucket balances and several different types of objects such as cubes, building blocks, vehicles, figures and so on.

What to do:
Model how to place objects into each side of the bucket balance so that they balance. The children should then freely explore the objects that will balance each other. Ask them to describe what they are finding out. For example, "three cars weigh the same as seven pebbles".
    Ask the children to make predictions.

Recording:
Ask the children to record what they discover in any way they choose.

What to ask:
Does that balance?
Which side is heavier/lighter?
How many more do you think you need to add to make it balance?

Words to use:
Balance.
Heavier.
Lighter.
. . . weighs the same as . . ...

To develop the activity:
You can use a number balance for free play with the children.
Use bucket balances in a shop in the role-play area.

Mathematical development

Age range	What a child is learning
Birth–11 months	Notices changes in number of objects/images or sounds in group of up to 3.
8–20 months	Recognises shapes in meaningful contexts.
16–26 months	Beginning to organise and categorise objects
22–36 months	Creates and experiments with symbols and marks representing ideas of number.
	Beginning to categorise objects according to properties.
30–50 months	Uses some number names and number language spontaneously.
	Uses some number names accurately in play.
	Beginning to represent numbers using fingers, marks on paper or pictures.
	Compares two groups of objects.
40–60+ months	In practical activities and discussion, beginning to use the vocabulary involved in adding and subtracting.
	Records, using marks that they can interpret and explain.
	Begins to identify own mathematical problems based on own interests and fascinations.
	Orders items by weight.

Active learning
Make sure all the children take turns in using the bucket balances so that they are all engaged actively at some point. If they are not physically engaged ask the children to make predictions.

Problem solving skills
Making predictions.
Noticing when objects balance.
Drawing on previous experience to find objects that will balance.

Encouraging discussion
Ask children to articulate their thinking to each other and predict what will happen when a child adds another object.

Links to prior experiences
When do they weigh objects at home – make links to baking.
Parents and carers may come into the setting to work on cooking activities with the children.

Possible misconceptions and difficulties
Not taking care over objects balancing. You may need to model this several times.

Subject knowledge for practitioners
Objects and amounts 'balancing' is a key aspect of algebra. If a child writes or draws 3 cars = 5 rocks they have written their first equation.

Personal and emotional development
Cooperating and taking turns in using the balances.
Making predictions activity.
Speaking about their predictions to the rest of the group.
Being confident to explore new objects
Working as part of a group

Activity 51: The car park

Setting up the activity: A play mat which includes car parks on a road system or a play multi-storey car park is idea. You can also make a car park by drawing grid lines on a large piece of paper or use masking tape on the floor of the classroom. I have even seen children using Cuisenaire® rods or other mathematical equipment to make 'garages'. You also need a large box of different sorts of vehicles.

What to do:
Play with the children in classifying the vehicles and placing them in different sections of the car-park describing the choices that you are making. For example, "This is for the blue cars." or, "This section is for trucks and this section for coaches." Encourage the children to join in making their own choices and describing the classifications they are making.

Recording:
Take photographs of a completed 'car-park' and ask the children to describe it – write down their descriptions. Children can count the vehicles in each section and record this in any way they choose.

What to ask:
What sort of vehicles can park there?
Where will this vehicle go?
Is there space for this vehicle?
How are these vehicles the same/different?

Words to use:
Same.
Different.

To develop the activity:
Ask the children to develop a story about the car-park telling the story as they play with the vehicles.

Mathematical development

Age range	What a child is learning
Birth–11 months	Notices changes in number of objects/images or sounds in group of up to 3.
8–20 months	Recognises shapes in meaningful contexts.
16–26 months	Knows that things exist, even when out of sight.
	Beginning to organise and categorise objects
22–36 months	Recites some number names in sequence.
	Creates and experiments with symbols and marks representing ideas of number.
	Beginning to categorise objects according to properties.
30–50 months	Uses some number names and number language spontaneously.
	Uses some number names accurately in play.
	Beginning to represent numbers using fingers, marks on paper or pictures.
	Compares two groups of objects, saying when they have the same number.
40–60+ months	In practical activities and discussion, beginning to use the vocabulary involved in adding and subtracting.
	Records, using marks that they can interpret and explain.
	Begins to identify own mathematical problems based on own interests and fascinations.
	Uses familiar objects and common shapes to create and recreate patterns and build models.

Active learning
The selection of vehicles and their movement into the car-park engages the children actively whilst thinking about classification. It also allows them to change their minds and reclassify without it feeling like a mistake has been made.

Problem solving skills
Exploring different classifications and making different choices
Exploring alternative arrangements

Encouraging discussion
Children should talk to each other about the choices they are making.
They should articulate their thinking to each other and ask the same questions that you have been modelling.

Links to prior experiences
Talk about the different vehicles that they see on the way to school.
Talk about parking near where they live.
Visit the school car park, talk about the properties of the vehicles – use this as a model for your own car-park.

Possible misconceptions or difficulties
Not lining up vehicles carefully in the spaces – model this process in your own play.
Compare the car-park with the school car-park.
Subject knowledge for practitioners
Allow the children to make their own classifications and listen carefully to their explanations. Discover their criteria by picking a vehicle and asking where it can park.

Personal and emotional development
Cooperating and taking turns.
Classifying the vehicles together and speaking about their ideas.

Activity 52: Growing towers

Setting up the activity: Use cubes or Lego® bricks that can connect together to create towers. You could also use Cuisenaire® rods to create staircases or cubes and cuboids building blocks. You will also need a flat surface to build on. If you have large cubes and cuboids to build with this is a great activity for the outdoor area. You could also set up a construction site in the roleplay area.

What to do:
Use the blocks with the children and all build towers. Create a series of towers that make a pattern. For example:

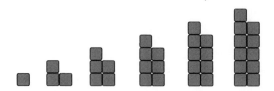

Ask the children what they notice about the towers you are building. They can then build their own towers to make patterns and describe them to each other.

Recording:
Take photographs of the patterns and ask the children to describe them. Write down their comments next to the images.

The children make drawings of their own patterns and make marks to describe them.

What to ask:
What is the same and what is different about the towers?
What patterns are there?
What would the next tower look like?
How high/long?

Words to use:
Same/different.
Pattern.
Bigger/smaller.
Next tower.
Length/height.

To develop the activity:
You can create models using the cubes. For example:

Mathematical development

Age range	What a child is learning
Birth–11 months	Notices changes in number of objects/images or sounds in group of up to 3.
8–20 months	Recognises shapes in meaningful contexts.
16–26 months	Beginning to organise and categorise objects
22–36 months	Recites some number names in sequence. Creates and experiments with symbols and marks representing ideas of number. Beginning to categorise objects according to properties such as shape or size. Notices simple shapes and patterns in pictures.
30–50 months	Uses some number names and number language spontaneously. Uses some number names accurately in play. Beginning to represent numbers using fingers, marks on paper or pictures. Shows interest in shape by sustained construction activity or by talking about shapes or arrangements.
40–60+ months	In practical activities and discussion, beginning to use the vocabulary involved in adding and subtracting. Records, using marks that they can interpret and explain. Begins to identify own mathematical problems based on own interests and fascinations. Orders two or three items by length and height. Uses familiar objects and common shapes to create and recreate patterns and build models.

Active learning
Building the towers using the blocks allows children to link the manipulation of the cubes to pattern building and recognition.

Problem solving skills
Planning the towers they build and constructing them.
Describing the properties of the towers.
Commenting on others' towers.
Deciding what the next tower will look like.

Encouraging discussion
The children talk about what is the same and what is different about the towers they are building.
Children discuss the patterns that they see.

Links to prior experiences
What sorts of buildings can the children see on the way to school? Do they have similar designs?

Possible misconceptions or difficulties
Some children may find it difficult to manipulate the blocks.

Subject knowledge for practitioners
Avoid the temptation to simply count the blocks. Listen to the children as they describe the patterns that they see. This will help them develop skills of subitisation as well as pattern spotting.

Personal and emotional development
Cooperating and taking turns to use the building resources.
Planning the towers that they will build together and discussing their ideas.
Working as part of a group.

Activity 53: Café seating

Setting up the activity: Use the role play area and set it up as a café. You will need at least three tables and 12 chairs. If you do not have the space set up a dolls café using dolls house furniture. This will mean you can use more tables and chairs.

What to do:
The children should decide how many people are going to visit the café. They then set up the chairs and the tables so that everyone can have a seat. Encourage children to find different ways to do this. The children then role play the café scene. They repeat the activity with different numbers of people.

Recording:
The children can record the seating arrangements in any way they choose. They can make marks to show how many people are in the café.

What to ask:
Why did you choose that way?
Is there another way to seat everyone?
Does everyone sit next to a friend?

Words to use:
How many at each table?
How many altogether?
How many more?

To develop the activity:
The children can provide the tables with eating utensils and plates and cups and saucers to explore other number patterns.

Mathematical development

Age range	What a child is learning
Birth–11 months	Notices changes in number of objects/images or sounds in group of up to 3.
8–20 months	Recognises shapes in meaningful contexts.
16–26 months	Beginning to organise and categorise objects
22–36 months	Recites some number names in sequence.
	Creates and experiments with symbols and marks representing ideas of number.
	Notices simple shapes and patterns in pictures.
30–50 months	Uses some number names and number language spontaneously.
	Uses some number names accurately in play.
	Beginning to represent numbers using fingers, marks on paper or pictures.
	Compares two groups of objects, saying when they have the same number.
	Separates a group of three or four objects in different ways, beginning to recognise that the total is still the same.
40–60+ months	In practical activities and discussion, beginning to use the vocabulary involved in adding and subtracting.
	Records, using marks that they can interpret and explain.
	Begins to identify own mathematical problems based on own interests and fascinations.
	Uses familiar objects and common shapes to create and recreate patterns and build models.

Active learning
The role play sets the activity in a real-life context and engages the children actively in their learning.

Problem solving skills
Exploring different possibilities.
Describing number patterns.
Exploring alternative arrangements.
Checking each other's solutions.

Encouraging discussion
The children should talk about their thinking and the decisions that they are making. They justify the choices they are making explaining why they think this is the best arrangement.

Links to prior experiences
Visit a café to look at the seating arrangements.
Think about alternative ways to organize the seating for school dinners

Possible misconceptions or difficulties
Counting to the required number. This can be carried out concretely using dolls and people so that they 'discover' how many people they can sit at a table by sitting one at a time.

Subject knowledge for practitioners
Encourage the children to experiment with arrangements before describing the patterns.
Look at the geometric patterns that are emerging as well as the number patterns.

Personal and emotional development
Planning the activity together and agreeing a seating plan
Taking it in turns to play the different roles.
Work as part of a group.

Activity 54: Hot cross buns

Setting up the activity: This is best carried out as a baking activity. The buns can be for any kind of celebration but need to involve some sort of topping. A hot-cross bun has two pieces of dough that cross on the top to create a pattern. You could also add a cherry on top or a sweet in each quarter.

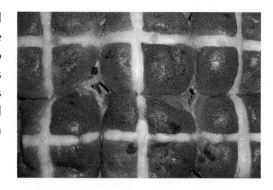

What to do:
As you make the buns talk with the children about the shapes and patterns that they see. Talk about how many strips of dough there are for each bun. Allow them to notice the patterns and talk about them. Encourage the children to think of other ways that they can decorate the tops of the buns.

Recording:
The children can record the designs in any way they like. They could also devise a way of sharing the buns out so that everyone gets a fair share.

What to ask:
How many buns?
How many cherries do I need?
Are there any missing?
How many 'crosses'?

Words to use:
Patterns.
Share.
How many?

To develop the activity:
Many different baking activities can be used for this type of activity.
Children can create designs for different types of cup-cakes.

Mathematical development

Age range	What a child is learning
Birth–11 months	Notices changes in number of objects/images or sounds in group of up to 3.
8–20 months	Recognises shapes in meaningful contexts.
16–26 months	Knows that things exist, even when out of sight.
	Beginning to organise and categorise objects
22–36 months	Recites some number names in sequence.
	Creates and experiments with symbols and marks representing ideas of number.
	Beginning to categorise objects according to properties such as shape or size.
	Notices simple shapes and patterns in pictures.
30–50 months	Uses some number names and number language spontaneously.
	Uses some number names accurately in play.
	Beginning to represent numbers using fingers, marks on paper or pictures.
	Compares two groups of objects, saying when they have the same number.
	Shows interest in shape by sustained construction activity or by talking about shapes or arrangements.
40–60+ months	In practical activities and discussion, beginning to use the vocabulary involved in adding and subtracting.
	Records, using marks that they can interpret and explain.
	Begins to identify own mathematical problems based on own interests and fascinations.
	Uses familiar objects and common shapes to create and recreate patterns and build models.

Active learning
By baking together, the children engage actively and problem-solve as a part of the activity.

Encouraging discussion
The children should discuss how they are going to make the buns talking about the process to each other.
    They can discuss alternative designs and decorations before agreeing which one they will choose.

Links to prior experiences
Talk about celebration cakes that they eat and how they are made.
What designs and patterns can they see on birthday cakes?

Possible misconceptions or difficulties
The children should carry out any counting and patterns spotting as a part of the making process.

Subject knowledge for practitioners
Avoid leading the children too much. Let them describe the patterns to you even if there are some inconsistencies in the buns. Discuss the similarities and differences later.

Personal and emotional development
Planning and carrying out the baking together.
Explaining the process to each other.
Working as part of a group.

Activity 55: Ways of making 6

Setting up the activity: You will need egg boxes and objects to place into the holes. These could be eggs or any other type of object. Use a range of objects in different colours.

What to do:
Set up a pattern in the egg box. For example:
Ask the children to talk about what they notice?
Create different patterns. Some of the patterns should not fill up all the holes. The children should quickly take over and create patterns for each other to describe.

Recording:
The children can draw the patterns that they see and make marks to describe the patterns in any way that they choose.

What to ask:
What do you notice?
What is the same about these patterns?
What is different about these patterns?

Words to use:
Pattern.
Full/empty.

To develop the activity:
Use different sized egg-boxes with 10 holes; 12 holes and 18 holes.

Mathematical development

Age range	What a child is learning
Birth–11 months	Notices changes in number of objects/images or sounds in group of up to 3.
8–20 months	Recognises shapes in meaningful contexts.
16–26 months	Knows that things exist, even when out of sight. Beginning to organise and categorise objects
22–36 months	Recites some number names in sequence. Creates and experiments with symbols and marks representing ideas of number. Notices simple shapes and patterns in pictures.
30–50 months	Uses some number names and number language spontaneously. Uses some number names accurately in play. Beginning to represent numbers using fingers, marks on paper or pictures. Compares two groups of objects, saying when they have the same number. Separates a group of three or four objects in different ways, beginning to recognise that the total is still the same. Shows interest in shape by sustained construction activity or by talking about shapes or arrangements.
40–60+ months	In practical activities and discussion, beginning to use the vocabulary involved in adding and subtracting. Records, using marks that they can interpret and explain. Begins to identify own mathematical problems based on own interests and fascinations. Uses familiar objects and common shapes to create and recreate patterns and build models.

Active learning
Creating their own patterns to describe and to compare to others engages the children actively.

Problem solving skills
Exploring and describing alternative patterns.
Noticing similarity and difference.
Generalising (all the patterns 'make' 6 in some way).

Encouraging discussion
The children should talk about their own patterns and describe what they are seeing.
They should also talk about other children's patterns.

Links to prior experiences
Do children have egg boxes at home?
How big are they?
Do they see any other containers at home which are similar (trays for baking cup-cakes for example)

Possible misconceptions or difficulties
Not 'counting' the empty holes as part of the 'sixness' of the container.

Subject knowledge for practitioners
This type of activity is a way of developing subitising skills. See page 000 in Section 1.

Personal and emotional development
Cooperating and taking turns in creating and talking about the patterns.
Listening carefully when others are speaking about their ideas.
Working as part of a group.

10 Mainly data handling

As with the previous chapter the English National Curriculum and the Early Learning Goals do not explicitly state objectives for data handling. I do think it is valuable for children in the early years to explore data handling activities not least because though these activities they will develop an understanding of the meaning of numbers when applied to this sort of an investigation. In the New Zealand curriculum there is an explicit objective under the heading of "statistics". This objective suggests that:

> Within a range of meaningful contexts [children] should be able to collect everyday objects, sort them into categories, count the number of objects in each category and display and discuss the results.

There is also an "exploring probability" objective which states that:

> Within a range of meaningful contexts [children] should be able to classify events from their experiences as certain, possible or impossible.

The first 4 activities that follow offer ways to explore the first of these objectives and activity 55 gives the children an opportunity to discuss probability within the context of the weather.

As these activities do not have any direct links to the English National Curriculum or the Early Learning Goals I have simply outlined the activities without any reference to English objectives.

Routine activities

Children will sort and classify objects without any encouragement. Just make sure that there are lots of different objects to sort and classify in the role-pay area and whenever the children are engaged in free play.

You can also model how to use tally charts to keep a running total of how many times events happen or to make sure that everyone has a turn in a game. Make this a regular part of your practice allowing the children to keep records in any way they wish.

Activity 56: The clothes shop

Setting up the activity: This could take place in the role-play area or as a part of class-room activity. You will need a range of dolls or figures (male and female) and a selection of clothing. This can either be real clothes or images cut out from catalogues.

What to do:
Ask the children to select a doll or a figure and describe the sorts of clothes that they like to wear. This could be related to colour, to pattern or to a particular style. The children can then sort through the clothes and select all the clothes that fit this category. They can then select an outfit for their doll or figure to wear.

Children can then sort all the possible items that the doll or figure could choose. They can also classify all the clothes according to a range of criteria that they choose.

Recording:
The children can place the items they classify into different hoops to record the classification. Take a photograph of this and ask the children to describe the classification criteria they have used. Annotate the photograph with their description.

What to ask:
Why are you choosing that item?
What is the same and what is different about those clothes?

Words to use:
Classify.
Criteria.
Group.

To develop the activity:
The children can explore how many different outfits they can create from the clothes that they have chosen.

Activity 57: The rock pool

Setting up the activity: This could take place in the outdoor water-play area or ideally on a school trip. You could also use a video or an image as a stimulus. You will need a range of toy animals which might be found in the water and place them in the 'rock-pool'. You will also need a net to catch the animals.

For a less messy (but less enjoyable) activity you could use a box and images cut out from magazines or printed off from the internet.

What to do:
Ask the children to take it in turns to catch an animal. After each turn they should say what is the same and what is different about this animal and the other animals that have been caught. When they have caught all the animals in the rock-pool they should sort them into groups according to a range of criteria that they choose.

Recording:
The children can place the animals they classify into different hoops to record the classification. Take a photograph of this and ask the children to describe the classification criteria they have used. Annotate the image with their descriptions and use it as for display.

What to ask:
What is the same and what is different about those creatures?
Which group would you place it in?

Words to use:
Classify.
Criteria.
Group.

To develop the activity:
The children can explore ways to classify lots of different animals.

Activity 58: Travelling to school

Setting up the activity: Create sets of images of people walking, cars, buses, bicycles and any other way that your children may travel to school. Create a large grid on the wall at a height that the children can reach. Label the chart, "Ways we travel to school" and place one of each picture next to the vertical axis.

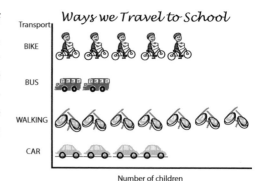

What to do:

Work as a whole class on this activity. Each child should take it in turn to come to the front and pick the image which represents the way that they travel to school. They should stick it on the chart at the front to gradually build up a pictogram of the ways that the class travels to school.

When the pictogram is complete ask children to talk to each other about what they notice. Allow the conversation to be as broad as possible. Remain neutral whatever the children say they notice.

Recording:

Keep a record of the children's discussion and use their conversation to annotate the pictogram.

What to ask:

What do you notice?

Words to use:

More/most.

Fewer/fewest.

Most/least popular.

To develop the activity:

The children could carry out the activity themselves in other classes and make comparisons between the results.

Activity 59: School dinners

Setting up the activity: Collect the choices for school dinners for the previous week and draw images of the food on a small poster along with the written 'dish'.

What to do:
Place the labels along a wall in the setting or preferably in a large space, outside or inside. Ask the children to talk to each other about their favourite foods; the sorts of food they eat every-day and the sort of food they might eat as a treat or for a celebration.

Share the labels and ask the children to discuss which of these items they would choose if they had to pick one. They should then stand in a line in front of the label of the food they have chosen

Ask the children to talk about what they notice. Allow the conversation to be as broad as possible. Remain neutral whatever the children say they notice.

Recording:
Keep a record of the children's discussion and use their conversation to annotate a photograph of the human bar-chart.

What to ask:
What do you notice?

Words to use:
More/most.
Fewer/fewest.
Most/least popular.

To develop the activity:
The children could carry out the activity themselves in other classes and make comparisons between the results.

Activity 60: The weather

Setting up the activity: Create large symbols representing different types of weather. If possible use the symbols that children might see on weather forecasts on the television or on the internet

Make three labels, 'certain', 'possible', 'impossible'.

What to do:
Ask the children to discuss the symbols and what they mean. Find out if any of the children have seen the symbols before.

   The children should take it in turns to pick a symbol and decide where to place it. They should make this decision after discussion with the rest of the class. When all the symbols have been placed collect the 'possible' pile together. Decide as a class which one you will select for the weather today. At the end of the day see how accurate you were with your prediction.

Recording:
This activity can be carried out every day at the beginning of the day and children can devise a way of recording how good they are at forecasting the weather.

What to ask:
Why are you putting that symbol there?

Words to use:
Certain.
Impossible.
Possible.
Most likely.

To develop the activity:
Have a thermometer available outside. The children can record the temperature during the day and compare this to the predicted temperature on the weather forecast.

SECTION

3

Appendices

Appendix 1
Glossary

This glossary contains all the mathematical terms that are used in the Early Learning Goals and the National Curriculum up to the end of Key Stage 1 (seven-year-olds). I have also added any terms which are used in the book and do not appear in either the ELG or the curriculum.

Units of measurement are described under the heading of the measurement they apply to. The names of common shapes appear under the headings of two-dimensional and three-dimensional shapes respectively.

Angle: Angles are measured in degrees. The symbol for degrees is °. A quarter turn is a right angle is ninety degrees or 90 °. There are 180 degrees (180 °) along a straight line which is a half-turn and 360 (360 °) degrees around a point or in a full turn.

Bar chart: A bar chart is a way of showing data simply.

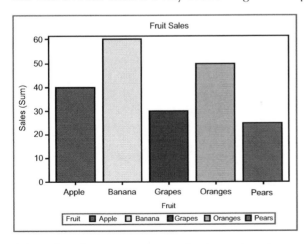

A bar chart has two axes, one horizontal and one vertical. Usually the objects that are being counted are represented along the horizontal axis and the number of objects on the vertical axis. All bar charts should have a title and the axes should be labelled.

Capacity: The terms capacity and volume are used interchangeably in the English curriculum. The capacity of a container is the maximum amount that it can contain. The capacity of a container is measured in litres, centilitres or millilitres.

The volume of a 3-dimensional shape is the amount of space that it takes up. This is measured in cubic centimetres or cubic metres (cm^3 or m^3).

Cardinal number: These are the counting numbers – one, two three, four and so on.

Clockwise/anti-clockwise: Used to describe the direction of turn. Clockwise is the same direction as clock hands move. Anti-clockwise (or counter-clockwise in US English) is the opposite direction.

CLOCKWISE   ANTI-
                             CLOCKWISE

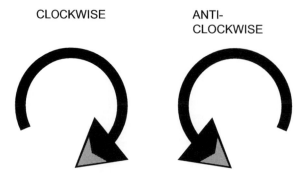

Continuous and discrete quantities: A continuous quantity is something that it is very difficult to out a precise whole value to such as someone's height or weight. A discrete quantity is something we can count like the numbers of boys and girls in a class.

Counting in multiples: Counting in a multiplication table. For example,
    2, 4, 6, 8, 10, 12 . . . is counting in twos
    4, 8, 12, 16, 20, 24 . . . is counting in fours

Count on/count back: If we count on the numbers get bigger each time we count. If we count back the numbers get smaller.

Difference: In mathematics this means the numerical distance between two values. So the different between 15 and 21 is 6 as $21-15 = 6$.

Discrete quantities: See continuous quantities

Estimate: This is to roughly judge what a number might be as in, "I estimate the hall could hold 150 people."

Equal/Equivalent: Two things are equal if they have exactly the same numerical value. This is the only time that an = sign should be used. For example,
    $3 + 5 = 8$
    $½ = 0.5$

Even number: An even number is an integer (whole number) that when divided by 2 leaves no remainder. This means that zero is an even number and that negative numbers can also be even.

Any integer which is not even is an odd number.

Fractions: Only one half ½ and one quarter ¼ are used in the English curriculum at this stage. One half refers to an object or a quantity which is divided exactly into two.

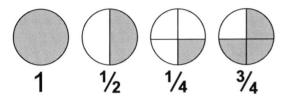

The number on top of the line is called the numerator. The number underneath the line is the denominator.

Length: The length of an object is measured in millimetres (mm), centimetres (cm), metres (m) or kilometres (km).

There are 10 mm in 1 cm

There are 100 cm in 1m

There are 1000m in 1 km

Mass: Mass and weight are used interchangeably in the English curriculum although they have different scientific definitions. Mass is a measure of the amount of material contained in an object. Weight is force exerted buy that object due to gravity. So, the weight of an object would be different on the earth and the moon whereas the mass remains the same.

Mass and weight are measured in milligrams (mg), grams (g) and kilograms (kg)

There are 10 mg in 1 g

There are 1000 g in 1 kg

Money: The denominations of the currency of the UK (Pound Sterling) are:

The four bank notes are: £5.00, £10.00, £20.00 and £50.00.

Multiplication and division facts: Often called 'times-tables'. All multiplication facts have related division facts. For example, the multiplication facts for 5 are:

1 x 5 = 5
2 x 5 = 10
3 x 5 = 15
4 x 5 = 20
5 x 5 = 25 and so on

The related division facts for 4 x 5 = 20 are

20 ÷ 5 = 4 and 20 ÷ 4 = 5

Number bonds (or number pairs): Most often number bonds to 10 are listed so:

1 + 9 = 10
2 + 8 = 10
3 + 7 = 10 and so on.

It is helpful to know number pairs for all whole numbers as this supports partitioning and helps children gain a 'sense' of number.

Number operations: The four number operations are:

addition +
subtraction –
multiplication x
division ÷

Odd number: See *Even number*

Ordinal number: Numbers that describe position. For example, first (1st), second (2nd), third (3rd), fourth (4th), fifth (5th) and so on.

Orientation: The orientation of something is the direction in which it points. For example, both of these objects are the same square. They are in different orientations.

Partitioning numbers: Splitting a number into two or more parts. For example,

27 = 20 + 7
15 = 9 + 6

Pictogram: Sometimes referred to as a pictograph. This is a way of representing data using pictures.

FRUIT	NUMBER OF CHILDREN WHO CHOSE IT
PEAR	🍐🍐🍐🍐🍐🍐🍐
WATERMELON	🍉
ORANGE	🍊
APPLE	🍎
BANANA	🍌

Place value: The place value of a digit is given by its position in a number. For example in the number

5 472 the '4' has a value of 400.

My Place Value Grid

Th Thousands	H Hundreds	T Tens	U Units	●	$\frac{1}{10}$ Tenths	$\frac{1}{100}$ Hundreds

Repeating patterns: Patterns that can be described by noticing the way that numbers or objects repeat.

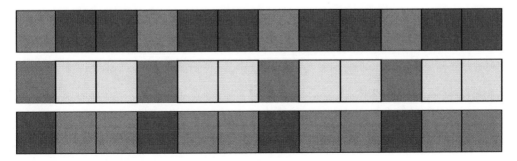

For example, in the top image the repeating pattern is one light, two dark, one light, two dark and so on.

Standard units: Standard units are the units that are used around the world to measure quantities such as metres, litres and kilograms. Non-standard units, such as hand-spans or cubes, can also be used to compare quantities.

Subitising: This is the ability to instantaneously recognise the number of objects in a small group without having to count them. You can probably 'see' there are 5 and 6 dots in the images below without having to count.

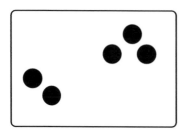

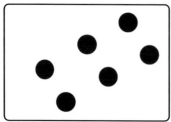

Sum: The total of two or more numbers. The amount we get when we add numbers together. Note: 'Sum' does not mean 'calculation'; it only refers to addition.

Symmetry: An object has line symmetry if you can fold the shape over a line so the two sides match exactly. This is also called reflective symmetry.

A shape has rotational symmetry if it fills the same space when you rotate it about a point before it turns through a full turn.

Tally chart: A way of keeping count of data. The tally chart records in lots of 5.

Time: Time is measured in seconds, minutes, hours, days, weeks, months and years.
   There are 60 seconds in 1 minute

There are 60 minutes in 1 hour
There are 24 hours in 1 day
There are 7 days in a week and 365 days in a year (366 in a leap year)
There are 12 months in a year
There are 10 years in a decade
30 days has September, April, June and November
All the rest have 31
Except February with 28, and 29 in a leap year
A leap year occurs every 4 years. 2016, 2020, 2024 are all leap years.

Time intervals: The amount of time between two events.

Three dimensional shapes: The curriculum includes cuboids, cubes, pyramids and spheres

Two-dimensional shapes: The curriculum names rectangles, squares, triangles and circles.

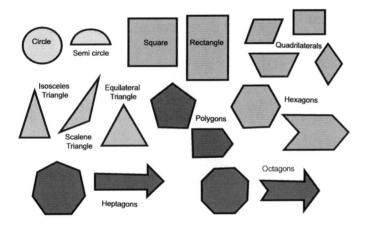

A polygon is a closed shape with straight edges.

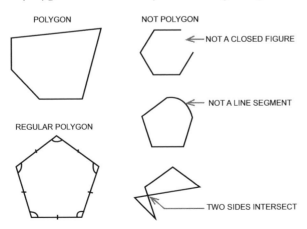

Regular polygons have all sides the same length and all angles the same.

regular polygons

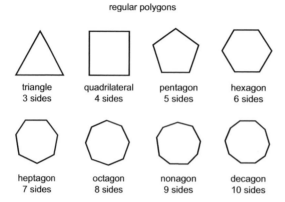

| triangle | quadrilateral | pentagon | hexagon |
| 3 sides | 4 sides | 5 sides | 6 sides |

| heptagon | octagon | nonagon | decagon |
| 7 sides | 8 sides | 9 sides | 10 sides |

Quadrilaterals are 4 sided polygons.

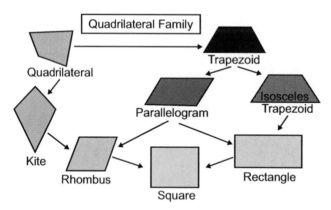

Turns (Quarter, half, three-quarter): See *Angle*

Volume: See *Capacity*

Weight: See *Mass*

Appendix 2
Useful websites and further reading

Websites

These are websites from organisations that early years practitioners have told me they find useful

Association of Teachers of Mathematics (ATM): https://www.atm.org.uk

There are resources available which are targeted at the early years such as 'Collaborative games and activities in the early years' and 'Cuisenaire: From early years to adult' as well as a journal which is published 5 times a year which includes articles written by early years practitioners.

Erikson Early Math Collective: http://earlymath.erikson.edu/

A site based in Chicago, United States, which aims to increase the quality of mathematics education in the early years. The site has access to recent research as well as resources for early years practitioners to explore.

Learning Trajectories: https://www.learningtrajectories.org/

Another site from the US. This is a web-based tool which supports early years educators in exploring how young children (birth to eight-years-old) develop their mathematical understanding. There are a wide range of activities available which can be used in early years settings.

Mantle of the Expert: https://www.mantleoftheexpert.com

This is an approach from drama in education which is directly applicable to early years education. The website contains free resources and lots of ideas for ways to use drama to support learning in the early years.

Maths through Stories: http://www.mathsthroughstories.org

This website, hosted by Dr. Natthapoj Vincent Trakulphadetkrai, suggests a wide range of books which can be used to support the learning of mathematics in the early years.

Montessori education UK: http://www.montessorieducationuk.org

This is the website for Montessori education in the UK. It contains links to resources and to training based on the Montesssori method

Nrich – Enriching Mathematics: https://nrich.maths.org

This site is based at Cambridge University and contains many activities to develop mathematics in the Early Years https://nrich.maths.org/13371 and articles which would be of interest to early years practitioners https://nrich.maths.org/11136

Reggio Emilia: http://www.reggiochildren.it/identita/reggio-emilia-approach/?lang=en

This is the website for the Reggio Emilia approach. You will find discussion of the approach, ideas for activities in the setting and be able to join a network of practitioners. You can also use this site to arrange a visit to Reggio Emilia. A must for any early years practitioner.

Further reading

Children's Mathematics: Making Marks, Making Meaning by Elizabeth Carruthers and Maulfry Worthington. Published by Sage publications, 2003.

This book draws on the authors' many years of teaching children aged three to eight years and their research with children in the home, nursery and school. The authors explain the development and range of young children's mathematical marks and visual representations, showing how children make mental connections between their own early marks and subsequent abstract mathematical symbolism, and go on to develop their own written methods. Combining theory and practice, this acclaimed book demonstrates how children's own mathematical graphics are highly creative and show deep levels of thinking.

Mathematics in Early Years Education by Ann Montague-Smith, Tony Cotton, Alice Hansen and Alison Price. Published by David Fulton, 2018.

The third edition provides an accessible introduction to the teaching of mathematics in the early years. Covering all areas of mathematics learning – number and counting, calculation, pattern, shape, measures and data handling – it summarises the research findings and underlying key concepts and explains how adults can help children to learn through practical experiences, discussion and more direct intervention.

Messy Maths: A Playful Outdoor Approach for Early Years by Juliet Robertson. Published by Independent Thinking Press, 2017.

This book offers ideas that will inspire you to tap into the endless supply of patterns, textures, colours and quantities of the outdoors and deepen children's understanding of maths through hands-on experience. Juliet argues that lots of outdoor play and engaging activity along the way is a must, as being outside enables connections to be made between the hands, heart and head, and lays the foundations for more complex work as children grow, develop and learn

Teaching and Learning Early Number by Ian Thompson. Published by Oxford University Press, 2008.

This book provides an accessible guide to a wide range of research evidence about the teaching and learning of early number.

Understanding and Teaching Primary Mathematics by Tony Cotton. Published by Routledge, 2016.

This book combines pedagogy and subject knowledge to build confidence and equip practitioners and teachers with the skills and knowledge to successfully teach mathematics to children of any age. The 3rd edition has been updated to reflect the latest research developments and initiatives in the field, as well as key changes to both the UK National Curriculum and International Baccalaureate, including a chapter on 'Algebra' and a greater focus on the early years.

Appendix 3
Resources

As I emphasised in the main text of the book the most important resources that you can use to support children in developing their mathematical understanding are every-day objects. This illustrates the notion that we are engaged in mathematical activity in many ways throughout the day and that we do not need special equipment to 'do' mathematics.

So, make sure that your setting contains lots of scrap modelling materials. Old boxes of all shapes and sizes, fabrics and patterns that have been recycled and different shapes of containers for filling and emptying in the water play area as well. Additionally it would be helpful to have the following resources available.

 Number

There should be large and small number lines on the walls and on the tables and painted on the walls and floor outside. These number lines should include zero.

Always make sure there are images with numbers on them on display. These numbers should include 3-digit numbers as children will see these outside school.

Collect receptacles such as egg boxes or cup-cake making trays which create arrays. You can get egg boxes in 4, 6, 10, 12 and 24. All of these should be available for children to explore.

Buy sets of **Cuisenaire® rods** for the setting. These are available from http://www.cuisenaire.co.uk. This website also contains videos supporting the use of Cuisenaire® rods in the classroom. The book *Cuisenaire: From early years to adult* available at https://www.atm.org.uk/Shop/Cuisenaire—from-Early-Years-to-Adult-Download/DNL129 is also a useful resource which explores the use of the rods in the early years classroom.

Another useful concrete representation of the number system is provided by **Dienes blocks**. The playful exploration of these materials supports children develop an understanding of place value. It also gives them mental images of 10s, 100s and 1000s. These are available from most educational suppliers.

Numicon®, available from Oxford University Press gives children concrete manipulatives exploring numbers 1 to 10 initially. The use of this manipulative goes well beyond exploring number bonds to ten and there is a wealth of information at https://global.oup.com/education/content/primary/series/numicon/?region=uk

Shape and space

Make sure you have lots of different examples of 2D and 3D shapes for children to play with and explore. It is important that these include irregular shapes so that children experience the difference between regular and irregular shapes. There should also be lots of different resources that can be used for construction

Polydron provide sets of magnetic shapes that can be used for construction and for tiling. I think the magnetic polydron is easier to use in the early years. This is available from http://www.polydron.co.uk/magnetic-polydron.html

Finally, a selection of tiles for covering surfaces allow children to build growing (and tessellating) patterns. My favourites are available at https://www.atm.org.uk/shop/Primary-Education—-View-All/MATs-Isosceles-Triangles-Pack-of-100-Activity-Tiles/MATs-Giant-Pack-1800-pieces/mat015

Measures

Make sure that rulers, metre sticks, tape measures and measuring wheels are all available in the setting. Similarly, a range of scales including balance scales and digital scales should be available. You should also have containers in different shapes and sizes, some marked and some unmarked.

Make sure that there are analogue and digital clocks, which are accurate, in the setting and refer to them regularly.

Index

Printed in Great Britain
by Amazon

61411855R00136